THE SCOTTISH RAILWAY SCENE, 1973–2020

A PICTORIAL REFLECTION

Inside Sleeve: A typical Sunday afternoon line up of Scottish sulzers on the back roads at Millerhill shed. It is 1985 and the BRCW class 26s and 27s are at rest awaiting the start of a new week's work. Rail blue is still the dominant livery. Whilst these locos wouldn't provide much chance of a 'cop' for the locals, they would delight visitors from South of the Border. That said, the Eastfield class 27/0s were not particularly common sights in Edinburgh. Of course, rail blue, class 26 s and 27s and Millerhill diesel depot are all now history. More recently a new depot for ScotRail emus has been constructed further down the yard from where the diesel depot had been.

Rear Cover Middle Right: A visit to the West Highlands often began with a stop at Crianlarich and perhaps a visit to the excellent tea rooms that were on the station platform. Eastfield's 37 402, *Oor Wullie* arrives on a passenger service. It is sporting the popular large logo livery with the Scottie Dog emblem of its home shed. All too typically of such trips, the weather was not great.

Rear Cover Middle Left: Class 26, 26 004 formerly D5304, has been refurbished and sports coal sector livery. It is employed on a coal working from Blindwells open cast colliery to Leith Docks and is seen within the docks complex. Several class 26s were fitted for merry go round working and this particular flow was a regular duty for the class. Changed days now however, the rails are still in place, but it is some time since any freight reached Leith Docks.

Rear Cover Top Left: What was once the multi lined entrance to Millerhill Yard has now only two tracks. The A1 trunk road crosses over the line and on the other side of the road will be built Newcraighall Park and Ride. A class 47 in ScotRail livery is en route to Millerhill. It was not all that common to see one of the push pull fitted 47/7s on more humble freight duties, especially when the sets were in use to Aberdeen as well as the Edinburgh to Glasgow flagship service.

Rear Cover Top Right: The sun has come out after some quite heavy rain and we find 47 490, *Bristol Bath Road*, formerly D1725 and went on to become 47 768, in the RES sector, and carry the name *Resonant*. The loco is a visitor from the South. It is on a push/pull set DBSO with some intercity liveried coaches which match the loco. Given the platform, this will most likely be for Aberdeen. Note that the North British Hotel (now the New Balmoral Hotel) is covered up whilst extensive stone cleaning took place to remove the grime from the steam age.

Front Cover: In 1985 Perth was host to a rail fair. It attracted several visiting locomotives, steam and diesel, as well as track machines and other rolling stock. Deltic *Royal Scots Grey* was one of those locomotives and is seen here in Perth station together with the station pilot 08 827. The Deltic was in almost 'ex works' condition and makes a fine sight. The Jubilee that attended remained in the carriage shed at the station for some time after the show.

Rear Cover Lower: A typical Sunday line up at Grangemouth shed of class 37s and 27s all still in rail blue but some of the 37s have the large logo variant. The building which was the old steam shed 65F has been demolished but the site is still in railway use.

THE SCOTTISH RAILWAY SCENE, 1973–2020

A PICTORIAL REFLECTION

JOHN BURNETT KIRK

PEN & SWORD
TRANSPORT

AN IMPRINT OF PEN & SWORD BOOKS LTD.
YORKSHIRE – PHILADELPHIA

First published in Great Britain in 2023 by
Pen and Sword Transport
An imprint of
Pen & Sword Books Ltd.
Yorkshire - Philadelphia

ISBN 978 1 39901 118 1

Typeset in 11/13 Palatino by SJmagic DESIGN SERVICES, India.

Printed and bound by Printworks Global Ltd, London/Hong Kong.

Pen & Sword Books Ltd incorporates the imprints of Pen & Sword Books Archaeology, Atlas, Aviation, Battleground, Discovery, Family History, History, Maritime, Military, Naval, Politics, Railways, Select, Transport, True Crime, Fiction, Frontline Books, Leo Cooper, Praetorian Press, Seaforth Publishing, Wharncliffe and White Owl.

For a complete list of Pen & Sword titles please contact

PEN & SWORD BOOKS LIMITED
47 Church Street, Barnsley, South Yorkshire, S70 2AS, England
E-mail: enquiries@pen-and-sword.co.uk
Website: www.pen-and-sword.co.uk

or

PEN AND SWORD BOOKS
1950 Lawrence Rd, Havertown, PA 19083, USA
E-mail: Uspen-and-sword@casematepublishers.com
Website: www.penandswordbooks.com

CONTENTS

INTRODUCTION

I am told that the Manse – my father was a Church of Scotland Minister – in Dysart is visible from the Main Line just north of Kirkcaldy, if you know where to look; however, I have no recollections of Dysart. The Manse in Forfar was at the other side of the town from the railway. I do recall the station there, mainly because we passed it on the way to Station Park to watch Forfar Athletic of a Saturday afternoon. I have vague memories of catching the train there but knew nothing of the swansong of the A4s which passed through the town daily in the mid-1960s. Today, except for the football ground's name, you might not think there had been a railway there. However, one or two over bridges are still clearly railway structures and happily Forfar shed still stands and is in industrial use.

As a family we used to go to Edinburgh to visit relations and friends of my parents and I can recall seeing the coaling stage of 63A whilst passing through Perth by road. Of course there was no M90 in those days, so the journey took us via Glenfarg. A couple of rail journeys stick in my mind; one to Hawick, as my mother's family hailed from that area and the second to Stafford to visit relatives and I think for that journey we travelled from Edinburgh Princes Street. It was not until we moved to Edinburgh in 1970 that my interest in railways began.

The Manse looked out onto the South Suburban line just east of Morningside Station and at that time was a very busy railway. It was also quite loud at times as there is a significant climb to the summit at Morningside in either direction, although westbound freights could be heard from a much greater distance and on occasion from almost a mile away. Many of the locos were still in green and at night some seemed to have flamethrowers for exhausts (the ill-starred Clayton Class 17s). A couple of years passed and then my friend from two doors along and I started taking the engine numbers and then our Saturday morning visits to Edinburgh Waverley began and that was it. The Ian Allan books were acquired and underlined. I am still in touch with the small band that frequented platforms 15/16 at Waverley of a Saturday morning.

Whilst the 'sub' and trips to Waverley provided the staple fare it wasn't long before trips to Haymarket and Millerhill were made and that in turn led to ventures further afield often by organised trips with the Scottish Railfans Society locally and to much more exotic locations South of the Border. There was another enthusiasts' club, 'Dalescroft', who also organised spotting trips. Like many enthusiasts, those early years sparked an interest for me that has been lifelong. Whilst the interest has come and gone over the years it remains and I have become involved in preservation, firstly at Prestongrange, where we operated a unique Grant Ritchie 0-4-2 steam engine. I wanted to try my hand at something bigger so went on one of Clive Groome's five day courses at the Bluebell Railway and what a fascinating, educational and inspiring course that was.

As a direct result I signed up with the NYMR as a cleaner and progressed through the grades to Fireman. I have never put myself forward for driving as, in my view, I am not at the railway often enough to maintain the extensive knowledge and skills required of a driver. There is no doubt that the line between Grosmont and Pickering is a real challenge for firing and I have had the opportunity to fire a wide selection of locomotives. Extension to Whitby has added another level of skills required and knowledge of the RSSB Rule Book. Through my good friend Pete Hanson, then a driver at the Moors, I was invited to join West Coast's support crew. That has given me some wonderful experiences including steaming past my house on the footplate of Jubilee *Galatea* on our way from Joppa to Perth as part of a 'Great Britain' charter and working with Frank Chippendale who used to fire for Clive Groome at Nine Elms. It is a small world!

Taking photographs was part and parcel of railway enthusiasm. Of course, as I suspect we all did, I tended to record the unusual rather than the ordinary on home territory so, as an example, I have no pictures of the 27s on the Edinburgh to Glasgow push pulls (or 'speed ups' as we called them). I started out with a Kodak instamatic, which was quite limited. I moved on to a 35mm 'point and shoot' which was similarly dependent on good light and a not-too-quickly-moving subject. I tried a couple of rolls of film with a Voigtlander Vito B that was in the house, but I couldn't get the shutter speed or aperture settings right. Finally, I was able to buy an SLR, a Fujica STX 1N, which I still use today. I also bought with it a 35-70mm lens which gave a great deal more flexibility and later on a zoom lens. Filmwise, I started out with slides, occasionally took black and white and then for a while took colour prints. When I bought the SLR I went back to taking slides, usually Kodak or Fuji films. Somewhere along the line I reverted to colour prints.

I never detailed what I had taken photographs of as some folk do. As a consequence, I cannot be sure of the dates of the images, unless the processor has added a date to the slide mount or back of the print. The locations and subject matter I am more confident about although I confess that whilst looking through my photographs I did come across a couple that I couldn't place and one where I still cannot work out where I could have been standing to take the picture. I have tried to provide what information I can but as some of these pictures were taken over forty years ago, please forgive any lapses in memory that may have crept in. Unfortunately, some of my earlier photos had been stored in my parents' garage which turned out not to be as weather proof as it should have been and the negatives and prints have suffered water damage.

There have been periods of time when no photographs were taken. I think we all go through such phases. As an example, I don't think I ever used a camera whilst in Aberdeen. There are also parts of Scotland that I visited only infrequently and not with a camera, the Glasgow sheds being a prime example. I do recall visiting Polmadie when the 50s were front line WCML traction. I was always quite lucky at obtaining permits for shed visits (even for Carlisle Kingmoor) but perhaps that was down to my using the Manse headed notepaper to make the application! As a result, this collection of pictures is not a comprehensive study geographically or historically.

I have tried to select images that reflect what the railway scene was at the time I was watching it. Much of the rolling stock, infrastructure and liveries have changed. Some of the locations are no more or have contracted beyond recognition. I hope this collection provides an insight into the changes that have come about over the years. For some they will stir memories, for some provide an indication of what used to be and perhaps inspire modellers. Wouldn't the shed at Millerhill make a very fine modern traction layout that could cover periods from BR green and Rail Blue through to the EWS era? Going through my collection of slides and photographs has been fascinating and I came across images I didn't recall I had taken as well as calling to mind events long forgotten. I have enjoyed this journey through Scotland's changing railways as I saw them and I hope that readers too will find much to savour.

CHAPTER 1
EDINBURGH WAVERLEY

I recall some visits to Waverley prior to railway enthusiasm taking hold. The changes that have taken place between then and now are quite striking. The forecourt has been redesigned, vehicular access is very different and the track has been reworked more than once and new platforms have been built and of course OLE has been installed.

It was the early 1970s version of the station that drew a group of young lads to the west end of the station, platforms 15/16 of a Saturday morning. I joined that band most Saturdays - I played rugby at school so missed some weekends – to see what the morning would bring. We never stayed past lunchtime. In those days the 'Sub' was closed at the weekends, so any freight traffic had to go through Waverley. A regular was 4M45, which was a car train from Bathgate to Millerhill and then on down the WCML. This almost always produced a Midland Region class 40 so was often a 'cop' and occasionally a 'namer' and some of the nameplates were still on the locos in those days. When I started taking numbers, the usual fare was a lot of DMUs; Metro Cammells, Gloucesters, Cravens and sometimes Derbys. There was a service from Glasgow Central which often had a Derby-built set on it. Loco wise the ECML expresses were Deltics or 47s, the Edinburgh to Glasgow shuttles were top and tailed 27s, the Inverness trains were double headed 26s or a 24 and a 26, always Inverness engines with their snowploughs and headlights. The Aberdeens were 40s or 47s and 27s often appeared on Dundees. Again, 47s were the mainstay on the portions for Carstairs. There were station pilots, both Haymarket 08s and empty coaching stock workings were usually class 25s. 20s and 37s didn't turn up all that often and I do not recall ever seeing a class 50 on a service train. Peaks, either 45s or 46s were infrequent visitors too. There was a service from Leeds which sometimes had a 45 on it but it always seemed to be 60 *Lytham St Annes* – I wonder if the Holbeck foreman kept that engine spare just for that job. Class 31s were extremely rare and I can only recall ever seeing two of the class in Waverley, those instances years apart. Numbers were all pre-TOPS and whilst most locos were in rail blue, there were still a good few green locos about. Renumbering commenced and with some of the classes where renumbering didn't follow any form of numerical order it could be some time before we knew what the identity of the now TOPS numbered loco was.

As the years went by, 47/7s appeared on the Edinburgh-Glasgows in their, to my mind anyway, very fine 'ScotRail' livery, HSTs began to run the main ECML services and the Deltics started their decline. Loco hauled trains became fewer. TOPS numbering was completed and green locos became a real rarity. Re-signalling of the Edinburgh area allowed the Sub to be controlled from the new Edinburgh power box so freights could be kept out of Waverley at the weekends.

Electrification began, initially allowing services to come up from Carstairs with electric traction, usually an 86 and as it expanded the East Coast main Line went live and the HSTs shared those duties with 91s. EMUs began to appear and occasionally there were 'oopsies' when an electric unit was signalled onto a line with no wires. My platform end days came to an end in 1978 when I finished school and headed to university. However, visits to Waverley continued, and still do, especially when something unusual was known to be coming in. The station today is very different, much expanded and much busier.

Probably the most iconic locomotives at Waverley in my platform end days were the Deltics. Allocated to Finsbury Park (those named after racehorses), Gateshead (those named after English Regiments) and Haymarket (those named after Scottish Regiments) they were the front line motive power for the East Coast Main Line. I recall one night, prior to number taking days, I was in the station with my father and we walked up platform 1 to see 9013 *The Black Watch* waiting to depart for the south; quite a coincidence as my father's Army Cadet Battalion was part of that regiment. There were only twenty-two but some seemed elusive as their diagrams kept them on the night time workings. This picture is from the summer of 1978 and their days are numbered as evidenced by the state of the loco and it was about to work a secondary service.

Whilst Haymarket did have an allocation of class 25s, in my days none were of the later 'full window' style or 25/3. The local 25s were often employed on the empty stock workings to and from Craigentinny carriage sidings. This example, 25 286 allocated to Carlisle Kingmoor, is stabled across from platforms 10 & 11 as was, a common place in those days to find a loco. Today an extra platform, the new platform 10, has been built along half the length of this side of the wall which separated the main station from the Sub platforms. This siding remains and today may well contain an electric loco for the sleeper.

An everyday scene at Edinburgh Waverley. A class 40, no doubt one of Haymarket MPD's allocation, sits at the end of platform 17 having brought in a service from Aberdeen or Dundee. When I started going to Waverley, there were still barriers and ticket collection on all platforms and we had to have a platform ticket, although most of the ticket collectors didn't take them from us when we left the platform so it was only now and again that we would have to buy another. By the time this photo was taken, Waverley had become an open station with no barriers. Staff were still in BR uniform and litter bins were few and far between. Train information was via the video screens as can be seen here showing details of the next train for Dundee. It is interesting that the open station policy has changed back to barriers, but they are mainly automated. Waverley recently reverberated to the sound of a class 40 again as two of the class appeared on a rail tour, some forty or so years after this picture was taken.

Another picture from 1985 and I was getting used to using an SLR camera. The 27s will have been on Dundee workings, I think. The picture is from platform15/16 looking towards 17 which was the platform usually for the Inverness and Aberdeens. It was unusual not to have DMUs in the way to obscure the view. As these were loco hauled, a pilot was still needed to remove the coaching stock to release the locomotives from the buffer stops. The train information is no longer displayed on the red cased TV monitors that could be seen at each platform end. Today there is a large board above the entrances to these platforms with arrivals and departures. Loco hauled trains are very much a rarity now.

Normally the sight of a class 47 in Waverley wouldn't attract a great deal of attention from the enthusiasts on platform 15/16, however, this one most certainly did. 47 077 *North Star* was one of the original named class 47s all allocated to the Western Region, mostly to South Wales sheds so their appearance North of the Border was very unusual. If memory serves me correctly, this was only the second of these named 47s that I saw in Edinburgh. I note that the stonework has been cleaned and that news of a rare 47 has spread attracting quite a crowd. Well, no, those in Princes Street Gardens had no interest in *North Star* but were waiting for an appearance from *Flying Scotsman*! It was ever thus. We were far more interested in the 47.

I mentioned the West End pilot earlier for removing empty stock from the Aberdeen, Inverness and other loco hauled trains. The pilot, a Haymarket 08 and in this case 08 570, when not in use could be found in this siding and now and again a loco would be stabled here too. There was also an east end pilot, also a Haymarket 08. Of course when loco hauled trains ceased there was no longer a need for a pilot, and with space at a premium this siding was removed during one of the two major track reconfigurations that have taken place since this photograph was taken.

Class 20s were not all that common in Waverley itself although they were in and around the Edinburgh area. Haymarket shed had an allocation of class 20s. They were most often found as pairs coupled together in this manner so that forward visibility in either direction is good. It is not if you are looking down the side of the bonnet. This view is from 'Jacobs Ladder' a set of steps that take you up to Regent Road where you can look down on the east end of the station. Platforms 10 & 11 have been extended but no electrification as yet. I have a notion these 20s may have been on a rail tour.

Class 40s were a common sight and sound around Waverley both on passenger services and freights. Haymarket had an allocation of 40s and visitors from the Eastern and Midland Regions also appeared. You could recognise an Eastern loco as that region was the first to remove the honeycomb grille that covered the No 1 end radiator air intake, Scottish Region followed that practice, but the Midland kept them in place. These two had arrived on a rail-tour towards the end of the 40s days and are seen at the east end of the Suburban platforms (then 20 and 21). It was unusual to see double headed class 40s. Real heavy weight traction.

A typical scene prior to the full electrification of services from Carstairs is an ETH class 47, 47 641 *Fife Region* on Inter City liveried Mk2 air conditioned stock. Had this locomotive appeared in the 1970s it would have caused a stir as it was D1672 or 47 086 *Colossus*, one of the original named Brush 4s which were allocated to Western Region sheds. They did appear now and again usually on rugby specials when the Five Nations rugby tournament was on and Wales were playing at Murrayfield. When I started going to Waverley, the trains for the WCML were often a four or five coach portion but with the advent of electrification more and more services were full sets which avoided splitting and joining sets at Carstairs. The first stage of electrification has begun but note that the wires are only for one of the Mound Tunnels and a limited number of lines at the south side of the station and West Coast trains would use what were then platforms 10 and 11. It would be a couple of years yet before the East Coast was also electrified. The track layout was significantly altered in the mid-1990s when electrification of the station expanded. Further alterations have taken place since to create more platform space.

Whilst the Deltics were notorious for creating clouds of blue smoke whilst starting away, this HST is doing a fair impression. It is coming out of platform 7 and is in the original yellow and blue livery. Looking at the signals this may be an empty stock working as it appears to have a subsidiary signal. There are still carriages in the motorail dock to the left of the HST and adjacent to the extended platforms 10 and 11. HSTs of course became a very common sight indeed. I can however recall the first visit to Edinburgh of the prototype. Just as the Deltics ousted the A4s, so the HSTs would oust the Deltics. ScotRail now use shortened HST sets on routes that would have had class 170 units.

A service, most likely from Aberdeen, approaches journey's end at platform 17 of Waverley. In charge is 47 641 *Fife Region* which seems to be a regular in Waverley as we have seen this engine already. This isn't a push pull fitted engine but is coupled to a set which includes a DBSO and is in the ScotRail livery. The platforms show that it has been wet that day. The loco was named at Dunfermline in October 1986 and during its stay in Scotland was allocated between Eastfield and Inverness. By 1991 it had been re-allocated back to the Western region at Old Oak Common and the *Fife Region* nameplates were removed. With renumbering firstly into TOPS and then further sub classes, keeping track of some class 47s' identity wasn't easy. This loco had been D1672, 47 086, 47 641 and went on to become 47 767 and carried four different names.

I confess that the Edinburgh to Glasgow push pull services were such an everyday occurrence that I didn't photograph them and as a result I couldn't find any pictures of the class 27s working them and have very few of the 47/7s. However, in 1990 I did, and unusually opted to photograph the DBSO end. This is taken from platforms 15 & 16 looking to platform 14 which was and still is the regular platform for the Edinburgh to Glasgows now worked by class 385 emus. Once again it looks like it has been wet. The service was on the hour and half hour which was increased in more recent times to on the hour, quarter past, half hour and quarter to the hour. I had to commute to Glasgow from Edinburgh for some months and having become jaded with the cramped conditions on the class 158s found that there was a Virgin Trains HST which left at about the same time but went to Glasgow Central which was closer to the office than Queen Street.

Something else I rarely photographed were multiple units, mainly because we saw them every day. I should of course have recorded the different types that came and went from Waverley; Metro Cammells, Gloucesters, Cravens, Derbys and later on cascaded Swindon and BRCW units. I have a vague recollection of travelling on one of the Swindon units that used to work the Edinburgh to Glasgow service. In this picture, I am sure that I was in the station to see the two class 26s in 'Dutch' engineers' livery which were working a rail tour. The 'big head-code', as we referred to them, Derby unit is incidental but of interest. These units were allocated to the Glasgow area and this class 107 is in the Strathclyde PTE orange livery. In the background is the then North British hotel which had been stone cleaned as it was a very much darker colour when I first started visiting Waverley. It is still very much active but is now called the New Balmoral.

Class 50s were rare in Waverley and other than for a rail tour as this is, I do not recall seeing one on a regular passenger working there. They did of course visit Edinburgh on 4G72, Gushetfaulds to Portobello liner and light engine back to Polmadie quite regularly but that did not run through Waverley. This gives a good view of the east end of the station. Both Motorail docks have rolling stock in them and the egg-box-like building is the signalling centre. Where it is and the area that is becoming a car park used to be the goods yard and there was a footbridge from Waverley to the elevated road that can be seen above the signalling centre. This view today would also include the new Edinburgh City Council buildings, extended platforms and full electrification of the station.

Having pictured the West End pilot earlier, it is only proper that we see the East End pilot. This is a 1990 picture and the Haymarket 08 has been adorned in sector livery. It is sitting in the Motorail dock. During my regular trips to Waverley the east end platforms other than 7 were never in passenger use however the post office was very busy at that end of the station. Like so many pictures in this book the East End pilot is now history.

Another very familiar sight (and sound, now and again both the 10:00 for King's Cross and the 10:06 for Plymouth in platforms 1 and 7 respectively would be Deltic hauled so you heard four Napiers idling away close together) in Waverley was of course the mainstay of the ECML express fleet the Deltics. Often when the route indicator at the mouth of Mound Tunnel rolled to NLD, looking through the tunnels into Princes Street Gardens we would see that the indicator was for the loco for a London train and would either be a 47 or a Deltic. That said it took me quite a while to clear all twenty-two of them and my last was 9009 *Alycidon* which I finally bagged on Haymarket in the fuelling shed one Saturday afternoon. This image is from 2003 and we find *Royal Highland Fusilier*, now in the care of the Deltic Preservation Society, on a rail-tour, as I recall it was top and tailed. Both engines are running but only one has started to provide the usual exhaust smoke screen. Looking at the picture I can, in my mind, hear that so familiar engine note too.

Into 2004 and electrification of the station has spread as the ECML is now under the wires. This is the north side of the station at the east end looking from what was then platform 1. We can see the very front of a 170 unit in what was referred to as the ScotRail 'whoosh' livery. Class 90s were common visitors from the west on sleeper services and for a while were used in conjunction with former Virgin Trains coaches and DVTs on the North Berwick trains. Here we see 90 036, still in its sector livery, attached to a North Berwick set. It would have to run out of the station and set back into, probably, platform 7 to form its service. The lines in the picture used to be simple through lines however as part of the station's expansion platforms 1 and 20 are now adjacent to the North Loop.

When the WCML electrics began to run right through to Edinburgh, it tended to be Class 86s rather than 87s and then class 90s began to appear on the sleepers. This is another example of a local enthusiast not photographing the ordinary and I found that this is one of only two pictures I have of class 86s in Edinburgh. This example 86 231 named *Starlight Express* is in Inter City livery matching the coaches it would be hauling. It is waiting its next turn in what were the motorail platforms which became the normal place to hold locomotives stabled awaiting their next duty. Often the locos for that night's sleeper would be found here. As memory serves me, the starlight express was a short-lived attempt at a non-sleeper overnight service as well as a West End musical.

For once I did take a picture of a unit. These 'rat cabs' as we called them had been transferred north from the Eastern Region and were now working the Edinburgh to North Berwick services. This unit must be spare and waiting for the increased service at the rush hour. Commuting from North Berwick and the other East Lothian stations creates significant passenger numbers. It was common practice to stable a unit here. As we can see the wires are very much up and weeds are present in the four foot and trackside. For the avoidance of doubt, the structure to the left of the unit is the remains of Calton Jail and not Edinburgh Castle which is on castle rock above the west end of the station.

Another major reconfiguration of Waverley took place to enhance capacity and simplify the track layout in 2007 and 2008. Additional platforms were created too and more recently further work has been undertaken to create further platform space at the east end of the station. This shows the west end of Waverley taken from Waverley Bridge. The points in the foreground are for the 'Sub' platforms which were 20 and 21 but are now 8 and 9. Some of the platforms have been extended to accommodate longer or more trains. To the left of the picture, beside the wall was the siding for the west end pilot (as seen in image 6). The engineer's trains were top and tailed class 60s with 60 066 nearest the camera. 4 class 60s were in use and were based at Millerhill for the duration of the project. Class 60s were being run down at the time and as a fan of these engines I couldn't miss the chance of nipping down the town of a lunchtime to see and hear what was going on.

CHAPTER 2
AROUND EDINBURGH

Whilst most of my early number taking was from trains going by the Sub or at Waverley, there were other places that were well worth a visit in and around the city. An obvious place to go was Haymarket MPD, readily accessible by public transport. My visits were usually on a Saturday afternoon and a polite request to the foreman usually gained access. Changed days now! In those days, the sidings at the east end of the shed were occupied by DMUs and the repair line, which I'm told was often full with Claytons before they were withdrawn. A shed visit would produce some of the shed's allocation of 08s,20s,24s, 25s 26s, 27s,40s, 47s and Deltics and visitors of those classes, except the 08s, and occasionally others such as 37s, 45s and 46s although the peaks were relatively uncommon. It was also possible to sit on the banking of the old LMS line from Princes Street and watch what was going on about the shed and what was passing on the 4-track mainline.

St Margaret's, Dalry Road and Leith Central had all closed before my time so the other shed to visit was Millerhill, more of which later on. There were still yards in action such as Slateford and Seafield, but I didn't visit either as all that might be seen of a weekend would be a Haymarket 08. The carriage sidings at Craigentinny were worth a visit to watch the comings and goings. The Granton branch was still going but the traffic there was infrequent. The Granton branch runs underneath Ferry Road and within a couple of hundred yards there are two other railway bridges, one of which was the line to Scotland Street goods yard. But a sign of how much railway activity there used to be in the city.

It wasn't until later years and the availability of a car that I could go to vantage points around the city, especially those on the outskirts. Saughton was a good spot as the Glasgow and Fife lines were still running parallel to one another before the junction. Once they had split, Turnhouse was interesting for Fife trains and out near Ratho for the Glasgow line. For the Carstairs line, Slateford station or Kingsnowe were worth a visit.

Portobello had interest too as there was a Freightliner terminal there, not that it was a photographic location, and a spur led to the power station which had its own industrial diesel. The power station is long gone. The line from Portobello continued on to Seafield and Leith Docks.

Looking back, I wasn't particularly adventurous going about the city but then there was plenty of interest literally on the front door step, or more accurately living room window. Edinburgh had railways aplenty and to make sense of the lines and who operated them I have used the excellent National Libraries of Scotland maps website to call up the relevant OS sheets and more recently purchased some of the sheets most regularly used. Even in the years since I began being interested in railways, the system has contracted. The Granton branch has closed but there was still rail traffic to the Powderhall waste compactor but that too is no more. The 'bins' (Powderhall to Oxwellmains binliner) was a favourite freight for enthusiasts.

This is Slateford station and a class 107 unit, or 'Derby big head-code' as we referred to them, sporting the revised blue and white livery (they were all over blue when I started taking numbers) is departing towards Haymarket and Waverley. I suspect this unit will have come from Glasgow Central, a lengthy trip with very many stops. The station building is long gone now. The points visible provide access to the suburban line. It is a bi-directional link and behind the photographer is a cross over to allow east bound trains to access 'the Sub'. The line runs between Slateford yard and Meggetland playing fields (the home of Boroughmuir Rugby Club) joining the Sub proper at Craiglockhart junction. The line runs underneath the Union Canal and through the closed Craiglockhart station, it would very much be power on as you are straight into the climb to Morningside Station.

The DMU sidings at Haymarket seen from the embankment of the closed Edinburgh Princes Street to Barnton, Granton and Leith line which ran over the Waverley to Glasgow and Fife lines. We also see the depot's breakdown crane and coaches and the repair line (which on one occasion had an ex LMS Black 5 that was on Haymarket for attention to one of its wheel-sets after working on the West Highland Line) as well as a selection of units. These are mainly Metro Cammells which were the most common we saw and several of which were allocated here. There is a variety of liveries on view, the then standard blue and white, its predecessor rail blue and the orange and black of Strathclyde Passenger Transport Executive. These sidings would be emptied out at rush hours as the sets were strengthened for commuters. On shed we can just make out a 47 and a Deltic. On the running lines there is a class 27 on an incoming service probably from Dundee and an Edinburgh to Glasgow set which would have had a ScotRail liveried 47/7 on the other end. A very busy scene, and plenty of diesel fumes which may have been masked by the smell from one of the nearby breweries.

This is Haymarket Station and the class 27 is working an Edinburgh to Dundee service. The loco is sporting full snowploughs and the driver is leaning out looking for the tip from the guard. I discovered at Levisham on the NYMR that on a class 26 looking back for the guard's tip was a task for a contortionist and my foot slipped off the deadman's pedal. Haymarket has since been electrified, substantially rebuilt with a new booking hall and forecourt and had an additional dead end line, platform 0, put in just about where the fence is. What was the car park has been built upon and the Edinburgh Tram line runs nearby. I think the coal yard just west of the station was still in business then. Behind the wall on the other side of the station was a distillery which was a regular destination for a 26 and carbon dioxide tanks. That too is long gone and is now housing.

Back at Haymarket shed, 26 046 runs beside a class 101 DMU at its home shed. This had been an Inverness loco but transferred to Haymarket in 1973. The Haymarket 'Castle' emblem can be seen. The corridor doors and disc headcodes have gone but it is sporting snowploughs. These really do make hooking on and off a very much trickier task than it needs to be. Class 26s were staple fare on mainly freight working around the city and some examples were fitted out for coal traffic. Whilst Inverness used them for passenger work, often double-headed, they were not frequently seen on passenger duties in Edinburgh.

It is the last day of the Deltics in BR service some forty years ago. The Farewell Tour ran from King's Cross to Edinburgh and back. Here the loco for the southbound leg, 55 022 *Royal Scots Grey* is waiting on Haymarket shed. I think the foreman had given up trying to keep enthusiasts off the shed. It was a sad winter's day and in Waverley I witnessed grown men crying at the end of Deltic traction. Of course Deltics have run again on the main line but as preserved engines. This photo was taken using the Vito B and I was struggling with the exposures; that said, it was a very dull day.

The same day and in the running shed at Haymarket we find the loco from the north bound leg 55 015 *Tulyar*. It ran light engine south after the Tour had departed Waverley. This was also taken with the Vito B which had a 'B' time exposure function and I was taken aback when the film returned from the processors at the result. I didn't have a tripod so I rested the camera on the fitters' metal table that was in the running shed and the image is a bit 'skweebiff' (squint) as the Vito B's case had a screw fixing at one end so the camera couldn't sit flat on the table. I have had a couple of turns on Deltics at NYMR and I would not have liked the secondman's task of looking after the steam heat boiler located in the middle of the engine room between the two Napiers.

Still at Haymarket shed but on a different day, most likely one of my Saturday afternoon visits, we find a class 27 in the maintenance shed. I don't recall just what was being done to the engine, but it was one of Haymarket's allocations. For those who like to cab locos this set up in the maintenance shed allowed easy access to the cab of whatever loco happened to be in for repairs. Being a weekend there weren't many of the fitting staff at work so you could look about the locos in for repair pretty much to your heart's content.

With the unmistakable shape of 'Arthur's Seat' on the skyline, this is the Edinburgh to Glasgow main line. I am not at all sure what service this 47 is working. The location is towards Gogar and the line has on one side a chicken farm and on the other a scrap yard. 47s really were very common on all manner of workings with several sheds in Scotland having an allocation of them over the years.

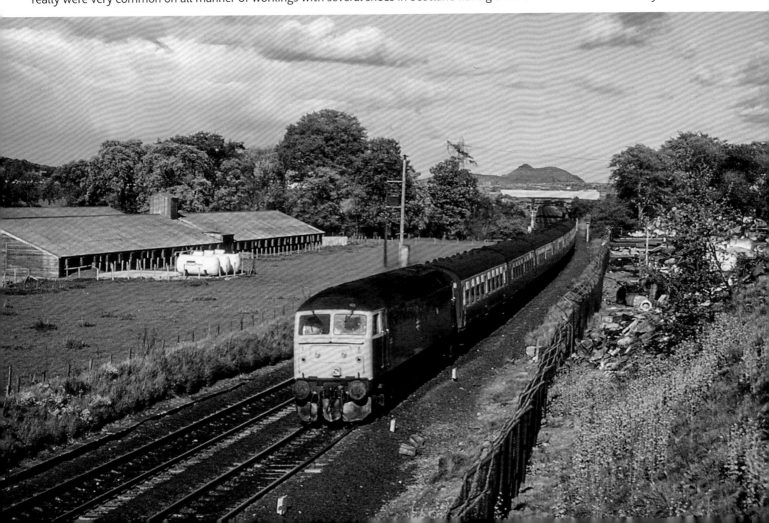

This is Kingsknowe station on the line for Midcalder junction where the line for Shotts, Uddingston (where the cement traffic from Oxwellmains goes), Mossend Yard and Glasgow Central diverges from the line to Carstairs. The unit is Swindon built. When I started taking numbers, we did not often see Swindon units in Edinburgh. The Swindon units that had been used on the Edinburgh and Glasgow services had been replaced by push/pull 27s. The Swindon units used at Ayr and between Aberdeen and Inverness did not appear in Waverley. This unit has been cascaded from use on the Central Wales line.

This Metro Cammell unit is heading west towards Slateford and Kingsknowe. The imposing building to the right of the lineside is the Caledonian Brewery. Edinburgh was once home to very many breweries and often, especially in the Haymarket area, the smell of that industry was strong. Whilst this brewery is still in production it has recently been threatened with closure. This line is now electrified.

This is Craigentinny, which was the carriage sidings and servicing facility for Edinburgh. With the advent of the HSTs their servicing was also done here and that progression continued with the 91s and DVTs, Voyagers and now Hitachi electric and bi mode sets. Class 25s were the usual traction for the numerous empty stock workings to and from Waverley. This scene however is well into HST days with two sets, but still in the original blue and yellow livery, in view whilst the ubiquitous class 47 is working an empty stock. Note that the fuelling point was also supplied by rail.

The Metro Cammell unit, which had been recently refurbished is running on the Fife lines and is near to Edinburgh Airport or Turnhouse as it was known before expanding into the major international airport that it now is. This unit has come from Fife and is Edinburgh bound. The real bonus of the multiple units was the view out of the front. Most drivers left the blinds up so sitting right at the front gave you an excellent view. Crossing the Forth Rail Bridge gave you a driver's eye view.

'Arthur's Seat' is on the skyline again and also, in this view, Edinburgh Castle. The Edinburgh to Glasgow and Fife lines run in parallel here before diverging at Saughton Junction. The class 37, in the 'Dutch' engineer's livery, is on the E&G lines, it is paired with stock in the Regional Railways livery and a unit can be seen on the Fife lines. This view wouldn't be possible today as the Edinburgh Trams run alongside and to the left of the railway and cross up and over the railway.

This is the fuelling point at Craigentinny. I doubt that nowadays one could get so close to the action at any depot. We see a Haymarket allocated 08 and, on a rail tour 45 106. Edinburgh remains a popular destination for rail tours and brings unusual traction to the city, in the last few weeks as I write, class 47s, class 40s double heading and 46115 *Scots Guardsman*. The 45 had been repainted into BR green with red buffer beams and other decorations such as the aluminium double arrow symbols and was a popular machine for rail tour work. It might have been a candidate for preservation, however it suffered serious fire damage and was scrapped in 1992. Peaks did appear in Waverley but not too often. I confess that 45s are personal favourites of mine.

A 1990 view at Haymarket Station. The class 47 is on a West Coast Main line working and on leaving Haymarket will turn left at Haymarket East junction and leave the city via Slateford and Kingsknowe. Apart from the sleepers, seeing a loco hauled train at Haymarket today would be a rare event indeed. The loco is sporting the 'large logo' livery which took over on some locos from the plain rail blue. Behind the station wall used to be a distillery which was rail connected but that area is now housing.

I am not sure why I had been in the car park of Meadowbank Stadium (which has recently been demolished and rebuilding is ongoing) but I noticed this item sticking out of the ground. The railway is the East Coast Main Line and the office block in the background is St Margaret's House. That office block and the one behind it were built on the site of 64A St Margaret's loco shed and the Meadowbank velodrome was built on the other side of the main line where the dock pilots were stabled in steam days. The item is of course the end of a fire iron which must have been discarded from 64A. It was an odd thing to see and I thought worth recording.

A Swindon built DMU heads west on the Edinburgh to Glasgow line in the Ratho area. There was a chicken factory in the area so hanging around to take photographs could be an unpleasant time. However, traffic on the line was, and still is, quite plentiful. Swindon units were used on the Edinburgh to Glasgow Queen Street services before the introduction of the push/pull class 27s. By the time this picture was taken, the class 47/7s were in charge of the Queen Streets. This unit is a class 120 and was cascaded to Scotland from Wales, the Edinburgh to Glasgow Swindon built units were class 126.

Never a common sight in Edinburgh, class 45s did appear from time to time. However, this was a charter using a now preserved 45 112 *The Royal Army Ordnance Corps* and the crew have obligingly set the head-code for the special; 'one zulu two one'. It was a holiday in Stafford and a West Midlands rover ticket which allowed me to travel behind 45s on front line passenger duties and make them one of my favourite locomotives. A fine sight and sound and, as I discovered at NYMR, a very flexible and capable loco. One of the shed staff described a visiting 45 that he had been shunting with as 'an amiable cart horse'. 45 112 however was just getting into its stride as it accelerates away from the city again at Slateford but note that the station building is no more and that the route is now electrified.

This picture shows the empty binliner returning to Powderhall from Oxwellmains known locally as "the bins". The wagons look very clean which suggest they may be quite new. A class 47 in sector livery is in charge. To the right of the line, the flats that are there now have not been built and to the left is the back of Macdonald Road Fire Station which had mock up ship superstructure used for training purposes, however, it is no more. This is a winter's morning going by the quality of light and the apparent frost on the sleepers. In 1824, Edinburgh became the first city to have its own Fire Brigade under the leadership of James Braidwood, who then moved to London to set up a Fire Brigade there.

Fast forward several years and 47s are no longer part of the freight scene under EWS. Whilst the 'bins' are still running (they ended when the compactor failed in late 2017) the traction has changed. On this Saturday morning, as this was one freight which regularly ran at the weekend, 60 097 in EWS maroon and gold is in charge of 6B46. The 60 had brought in the now empty wagons, unhooked and was in the process of running round its train before shunting them into the loading area for filling. The loco would then uncouple and head back light to Millerhill from where it had come earlier in the morning. I think this must have been one of the last Millerhill jobs that wasn't a re-man of a longer distance freight. The bins was always a favourite with photographers, perhaps because of the traction or perhaps because it almost always ran to its booked time. As a big fan of Class 60s I was always pleased to see and hear one on the bins! The line now is out of use and heavily overgrown. To the left of the picture used to be Edinburgh Corporation Transport's Shrubhill works which used to have a museum where the last Edinburgh tram car 35 could be found. The site has been redeveloped and will be used for housing. Car 35 is at the Tramway Museum at Crich in Derbyshire.

The same freight working but this time looking from the same over bridge but the other way from the previous picture. 37 427 is in charge and is shunting the wagons back into the compactor loading area. When the compactor failed, the site was very quickly cleared and all that remains is the very fine red sandstone stables block. You would not know that this had been a refuse disposal site. Nearer the camera, construction work is ongoing to the right and to the left is the rear of Macdonald Road fire station but the ship has gone and the station itself is undergoing a major facelift. The bins could produce as traction a 60, 66 or 67 but for a while it was a 37 turn which again made it popular for enthusiasts and kept Millerhill men conversant with class 37s. Oxwellmains also took binliners from the Greater Manchester area. We will see the bins again in a later chapter on the ECML.

CHAPTER 3
LEITH

Until relatively recently, the residents of Leith considered themselves not to be a part of the City of Edinburgh. As an example, Leith Police were a separate force from the City's. Leith has its own identity and with the docks and associated workings was a must for the railway companies to serve. The copy maps I bought from the National Libraries of Scotland come from the 1930s and 40s so show which companies' lines are which. The LNER came into Leith from the east and the LMS from the west (the same line that crossed the Glasgow and Fife lines at Haymarket and the vantage point for watching trains at the shed and on the main lines described earlier)via Granton, serving not only the docks but an array of industrial premises and the proliferation of lines and yards was impressive. Without the OS maps I find it very difficult to navigate the various lines as there were so many. As an example, Leith North and North Leith were two different locations. Perhaps the most impressive statement of Leith as a distinct settlement and not just a suburb of Edinburgh was the vast Leith Central Station. Of course that was only one of several stations in Leith and only one, Leith Citadel, still stands and is in use as a youth centre. Whilst not a large structure, its Greek column frontage is eye catching. To gain an impression of just how intensive railway activity was in Leith I recommend a look at an old OS map via the NLS website.

I confess I didn't visit Leith as a railway location until much later but in the mid-1970s there was still a lot of traffic for the docks and some of the factories and mills still had rail connections. Seafield was still an active yard. Fast forward to today and the ex LNER line into the docks is still there although it is heavily overgrown and the footbridge at Seafield is no more. Coal, grain, chemicals and coated pipes used to provide traffic. Portobello power station is long gone too. The ex LMS lines too are no longer there, however signs of railway activity remain in overbridges and some of the docksides still have rails embedded in them.

I am glad that I did make a couple of trips to Seafield to record the remaining rail activity, braving the smell of the water treatment works and the cold into the bargain as both visits were on winter mornings.

26 004 comes out of the Docks complex proper, the wall, complete with Forth Ports Authority sign, marking the boundary. The train is coal empties, the load having been discharged previously in the docks complex for loading onto ships. As can be seen, the space is tight and a limited clearance sign is also visible on the wall. I doubt very much that you would be allowed to be in such close proximity to railway activity today.

Looking into the docks from the wall seen in the previous picture shows a class 26 working a coal train, the wagons being of the HAA family, and an 08 shunting tanks. In the background are various works creating a busy industrial scene. Leith Docks was still very active railway-wise with different flows including coal and chemicals. The railwayman has hi-vis clothing of the day, no doubt today that would require full all-over garments and a safety helmet. This is a scene that cannot be repeated today.

Taken from the vantage point of the footbridge, which is no longer there, we see a class 26 heading away from the docks and Seafield with its train of coal empties. There is also a class 47 on tanks which I think were chemicals rather than fuel. Again, there is a lot going on railway- and docks-wise. This is one of the pictures I was glad that I had gone out to take as all of this activity is no more.

47 361 *Wilton Endeavour* has an interesting load and is most likely destined to return to Teesside with this train. The loco was allocated to Thornaby and this view must be 1983 or later as the locomotive wasn't named until that year. 47/3s did work into Edinburgh but I cannot recall seeing many of them, certainly they were not common round the Sub but workings from Leith would go first to Millerhill and onwards from there so a working for Tyne Yard and further south would go out of Millerhill straight onto the ECML. This picture also shows us the footbridge which is no longer in situ.

47 361 is in the background and another freight has arrived bound for the docks, this time a pair of class 20s with a load of fuel probably from the Grangemouth refinery. This shows that this was still quite a busy location for freight activity and merited an 08 for shunting. Of course, even this activity is a shadow of what would have been moving around on rail in previous years. Today the line is still there, heavily overgrown and only very infrequently used.

A pair of class 20s at the east side of the level crossing, the nearest one with head-code discs, the further with head-code boxes, and they are coupled in the classic bonnet to bonnet configuration for improved visibility from either cab. One of the shops in the block of flats seen across the road was a cafe which must have been a very lucrative business at one time. Seafield was one of the locations around the city that I visited only infrequently. In steam days locomotives were stabled here over the weekend to lessen congestion at St Margaret's.

The view here belies the amount of railway activity that used to carry on in this area. To fully appreciate just how many lines were active in the vicinity, a study of the NLS maps website or the 'Locations' area of the 'Railscot' site would be of benefit. 26 004, which I thought suited its coal sector livery, has come probably from Blindwells in East Lothian with a loaded MGR. It will shortly arrive at Seafield where the crossing gates will be closed to road traffic to allow the train to proceed into the docks to deposit its load. The train is running on the remaining single line. That line is still there but has not seen traffic for some time.

26 004 has arrived at the crossing at Seafield. The footbridge I was standing on to take the photograph has now gone. The guard looks like his orange coat is not long out of its wrapper but it will soon lose that new look as he will have hooking on and off duties. From here the train will pass through what was a fairly substantial yard before entering the dock gates. These images are from the late 1980s after the locomotive had undergone refurbishment with the connecting doors plated up, the disc head-codes removed, asbestos removal and other mechanical work undertaken. 26 004 went on to receive the engineer's livery before withdrawal, however this loco escaped the cutter's torch and entered preservation. But only after further asbestos removal!

Taken in 2003, this view shows what remained of the Caledonian Railways terminus for passenger services Leith North. The station was served by trains from Edinburgh Princes Street. There was also a goods station, which was larger than the passenger one, situated to the left of the building in the picture. It closed to passengers relatively early in 1962, Princes Street station did not close until 1965. The passenger service was latterly operated by DMUs. Leith Citadel station is a few hundred yards east of Leith North on the opposite side of the road seen in the picture. Leith North's building survived for many years in industrial use but has been demolished and housing has been built. The road junction provides access to Ocean Terminal where the Royal Yacht 'Britannia' is berthed. Tram extension work is ongoing at this location.

This picture is one that I didn't realise that I had. It is taken from the north side of 'Arthur's Seat' and looks out across the Forth to Fife. We can see some parts of Leith Docks where Ocean Terminal is now and where the Royal yacht *Britannia* is moored. In the foreground is Easter Road Stadium, home of Hibernian FC. The stadium has been completely rebuilt since this picture was taken and there used to be a station to allow fans to be taken by train almost directly there. However, the main feature of the picture and demonstrating the sheer size of the building is Leith Central Station. Quite why such a large station was thought necessary isn't at all clear. It was never used to its capacity and when passenger services ceased it was used for coaching stock and then diesel multiple units and shunting locomotives as a depot, coded 64H. The station is long demolished, but this scene provides a fascinating look at the structure from a distance

CHAPTER 4
THE 'SUB'

The Edinburgh South Suburban line leaves the ECML at Portobello junction, along with the line to Millerhill. Today these are separate lines but in the 1970s they were not and the Suburban line split off at Niddire North Junction going on to Niddrie West junction through the yards there. There were also collieries at Newcraighall and Niddire which were both rail connected. Today the set up provides a useful triangle for turning steam locos; off the ECML to Niddrie West (a pretty stiff wee climb), reverse into Millerhill then proceed back to the ECML. Fort Kinnaird shopping centre now masks the industrial heritage of the area.

Onto the 'Sub' proper, Duddingston is reached where the branch for St Leonards Goods came off and that can still be used today but as a cycle- or foot-path and was known as 'the innocent railway'. It is also where the line starts to climb; there is a short dip from where Cameron Toll signal box was and then just before Newington Station the gradient increases again and it is a climb through Newington and Blackford Hill to the summit at Morningside Station. From there the line descends to Craiglockhart where there is a junction which takes you either to Slateford and the lines west or straight on to Gorgie and Haymarket, a tricky descent on a slippy rail! A full history of the 'Sub' is available from the Oakwood Library of Railway history OL139.

The line is a steep climb either side to Morningside where there was a yard and where bankers could drop off. There was also a signal box there which connected with Niddrie to the east and either Gorgie or Slateford to the west. The climb from Gorgie up to Craiglockhart is daunting and continues after Craiglockhart Junction under the canal and road bridges and into the cutting at Myreside and on up to Morningside Station. The climb from the east is longer and it was freights, particularly class 40 hauled, that in the 1970s I could hear pretty much all the way from Newington especially in the autumn when the leaves had begun to fall. You would hear the power go on, right up then off, a pause and then repeat and that would get a bit closer and louder each time until finally, at walking pace, the freight would appear, very occasionally being pushed by the following train. I wish I had been able to record the sound effects! I am told that an empty tin can was essential equipment for Millerhill men for hand sanding!

So, from the front window a young boy could see quite frequent freight trains passing including Claytons. Railway enthusiasm was only a matter of time. Millerhill was still quite a busy yard in the early 1970s and of an evening there were several, mainly long distance, freights. The local trips tended to be daytime workings such as the CO_2 tanks for the distillery at Haymarket, almost always a Haymarket 26. The local traffic as you might expect produced local locos but occasionally an Eastfield 27/0 might appear and to my recollection they didn't often venture east. It was the long distance workings that usually produced foreign engines and the Carlisle freight just after tea time 6M45 (I think) always had a Midland loco on it, often a class 40 and sometimes a namer and occasionally still with the nameplates. There was also an evening Oxwellmains to Uddingston cement and that often produced a Gateshead 46.

Walking home from school took me over the footbridge at Morningside Station where you could see the Up home starter (a semaphore with two arms, one at the normal height and one at cab height) and the Down colour light. There was a freightliner working 4G72 Gushetfaulds to Portobello then back light engine to Polmadie which appeared just about this time. It was a fill in turn for a Polmadie engine and could produce a 47 or a 45 but most often a 50. These were not at all common in Waverley but were often round the Sub. Indeed, there was a Dalzell to Lackenby steel working that also produced a 50 from time to time. So I saw most of my 50s on the 'Sub'.

The variety of freight was impressive, but the frequency began to wane. The line wasn't open at weekends but occasionally it was specially opened for diversions and passenger trains would appear. In the mid-70s, Edinburgh was undergoing re-signalling with control being centred at the new power box at Waverley. Morningside Road box was closed towards the end of the project and as luck would have it the son of one of the signalling engineer was in my class at school so I was able to purchase the panel (at scrap value £2.46) which is in quarter inch plate and two sections and weighs quite a bit. Three years or so back, one of the box nameboards appeared in a local auction house so I acquired that too.

The frequency of freights declined steadily but use as a diversionary route increased. However, in 1985 I moved to Perth and was no longer able to observe workings on the line. Years later when I moved back to Edinburgh, my flat was close enough to hear the trains but not see them and a subsequent move allowed me to see and hear the traffic. A favourite service to see and hear was the Lackenby to Dalzell loaded steel, a class 60 turn and one morning I witnessed a 60 restart the steel from Newington; quite a feat given the weight of the train.

Nowadays the line carries cement, intermodals, nuclear flasks, the alcans for Fort William and engineer's trains. It also provides diversions for passenger stock, charter trains and light engine movements. The empty stock moves for the ScotRail class 68 hauled rush hour Fife circle extras also used to use the line. I still do a double take seeing a class 73 going by in connection with the Caledonian Sleeper services! There are regular turns for Voyagers, one at night is a passenger service, and occasional visits from HSTs, ScotRail class 170s and TPE and LNER Azumas. The Royal Scotsman appears quite often and recently the Royal Train too. Traction wise it is mostly 66s. The steel still runs but only occasionally and is 66 hauled and last year one slipped to a very noisy stand just about right outside my house. I did wonder just where assistance would come from and thought most likely Mossend. 2021 has been even worse and on consecutive days the loaded steel and an intermodal stalled on the incline and I heard 'assistance protection' detonators being exploded by the assisting engine. The following week I noticed that some freights were being banked. The cements were for a while Colas 60s but now are Colas 70s, 68s appear on the flasks and 37s still show face on the NR train and with West Coast Railways moves. Engineer's trains sometimes produce a 56. The most unusual loco I have seen on the Sub? You will have to read on to see it!

It is the summer of 1973 and the Kodak Instamatic records a 'skinhead' class 24 reach Morningside Station on a cement train probably for Uddingston. Both platforms are still in place and the station buildings can be seen. Morningside Road's signal 17, the Up home is also seen; note the two arms. This cement has just climbed from Newington, a stiff test for locomotives and in the early hours one morning a similar locomotive expired a couple of hundred yards east of this location and caught fire. I got up and went out to see what was going on. I found a row of very tired and dirty firefighters sitting on the kerbside having been inside the loco's engine room to fight the fire. I asked if there was anything I could do to help and was given the biggest teapot I have ever seen to be filled with boiling water to make a brew. It took two kettles and two pans of water to fill it. Having negotiated the engine room of a 24 at NYMR in engineman's gear I hate to think how it must have been for the fire crew; pitch dark, wearing boots, yellow wet legs (that melted when you got them hot enough) heavy woollen tunics, breathing apparatus and those awkward shaped helmets! No wonder they were tired and in need of a brew!

Morningside Road signal box from the yard behind the box which is now covered with housing as we will see in picture 56. These sidings were well used in steam days, often for bankers. I managed to spend a Friday night in the Box which was most illuminating as to just how much traffic used the line at night. A lot from Millerhill up to just after midnight, then a lull until about 2am when freights from further afield started to arrive from the west via Slateford. One of those was a freightliner from Nottingham for Portobello and that explained why most Sundays there was a 45 or 47 from that division on Millerhill. The box was linked to Gorgie and Slateford boxes to the west and Niddrie to the east. Most of the signals were none too difficult to pull, however the Up distant, lever 13, was hard work! This picture was taken, again with a Kodak Instamatic, in early 1976 so the boxes' days were by then numbered.

When the South Suburban line was re-signalled and control taken over by the Edinburgh Signalling Centre, I was able to buy the panel from Morningside Road. The proviso was that I had to go and remove it from the box. I hadn't realised that it was in two pieces and of quite thick metal so was quite a weighty item. The lever description plates were just going to be binned so I also collected them and the signal lever number plates although a couple had disappeared already. Happily, the one for number 13 – the Up distant – was still there, showing that to clear 13 you first had to clear 15,16 and 17. Obtaining one of the boxes name boards many years later was a bonus.

A class 26, 26 004, has climbed from Craiglockhart through the cutting at Myreside to reach Morningside. The working is an engineer's train. The yard that used to be there is now gone and a start to the preparing the ground for building the flats that now stand here has just begun. The signal box too has gone as has the colour light signal that stood near where the relay box in the picture is. The allotments still seem to be well kept but they are no longer active today although the footbridge that this picture was taken from is still in situ and in use. This used to be a point for taking water on steam trips but to reach the hydrant you had to climb onto the footbridge and run the hose across the adjacent road to set into the hydrant. No easy task, so more recently we have watered via a tanker.

A view from almost an identical position as the previous picture but fast forward to 2011. As can be seen, whilst the Up platform is still there, building work has taken place and the area where Morningside yard and signal box were is now covered by housing. The train is one of Freightliner's class 66s on a coal working. Note that the HAA family of coal wagon has been replaced by a higher capacity design. Whilst similar locomotives appear now on engineer's trains, there are no more coal workings and there is a livery change ongoing for Freightliner locos, so even though this is a relatively modern image it too is now historic.

The Sub can be a useful diversionary route. Indeed, it was recently used to allow LNER services to travel south via Carlisle due to engineering work on the East Coast so Hitachi electric and bi mode units, coupled together as the Sub is not electrified, were seen over several weekends. Going back some years we find a 'Brush 4' 47 593 on a diverted service. It has come off the main line at Portobello Junction and is climbing up to Niddrie West junction. This is quite a steep climb and as can be seen quite a tight curve. Today this is a bi-directional single line however in the 1970s it was double track and the train would shortly run through what had been a not insignificant goods yard. There is no trace of this yard remaining today. Over the years I have seen all manner of locos on diversions round the Sub including Deltics.

This shows us Niddrie West Junction. Class 47, 47 630 has come from Portobello Junction and is about to go on to the suburban line proper. Light Engine movements were still quite common at the time. The lines in the foreground go to Newcraighall and Millerhill. This forms a useful triangle for turning steam engines. The engine could pass through Niddrie West, reverse to Millerhill and then proceed back through Newcraighall and back to Portobello. There were collieries nearby, a brewery at Duddingston and from there the branch went to St Leonards where there were bonded warehouses. That branch, known as 'The Innocent Railway', closed in the '60s; however, the track bed is now a cycle path. This freight activity meant that there used to be a yard here which was still in use in the early '70s as I recall. Given the nature of much of the freight, theft was a real problem in the yard.

A much more recent picture taken from the over bridge at Oswald Road, between Blackford Hill and Morningside Road. ScotRail decided to augment its rush hour Fife Services with two loco hauled sets. Latterly these were provided by DRS using class 68s and Mk2 coaches. The coaches and some of the locos received Scot Rail livery. These trains were stabled in the Motherwell area, so morning, afternoon and evening there were empty stock moves to and from their base. The contract ended in 2020 so these workings are no more. Given the light, this is an afternoon picture, so this is either 5G13 or 5L69 Motherwell to Edinburgh empty coaching stock. Class 68s still visit the Sub but working nuclear flask trains to and from Torness Power Station.

I mentioned the most unusual locomotive that I have seen on the suburban line and here it is, a class 52 'Western'. This view is taken from the over bridge at Cluny Avenue looking east and downhill. The Western was North of the Border for a rail tour which also ran into Fife. Whilst the Western had no problems hauling this train up to Morningside, in Fife it did encounter problems on the climb from Inverkeithing to North Queensferry with some significant wheel slipping. This picture shows the tour with passengers aboard. It returned empty stock later in the day and went to Millerhill for servicing before continuing with the tour. The train is approaching signal ES 671 which is on the gradient up to Morningside Road. In the 1970s the next signal was at the platform end of Morningside Station. The next signal on the down line today controls Craiglockhart Junction so if the line through Slateford is busy this signal can be at red. This is not a place you would want to be stopped! I have seen a 68 on the empty stock restart from here; a lot of noise but no problem and I saw a 66 on an intermodal also stopped here and I suspect that the driver would be none too pleased with the signaller for halting the train on this incline.

Seeing D1057 *Western Chieftain* was such an unusual sight that it merits a second appearance. This picture is taken from the former entrance gate to Newington Station which had an island platform. The platform was still there when I first moved to Edinburgh in 1970. The Western is coasting downhill and is running empty stock to Millerhill. This is one of the locations we have used to take water on steam charters. One evening we stopped here with Jubilee *Galatea* to fill the tender for our engine and support coach working back to Carnforth. One of the shops now in the former station buildings is an Indian restaurant so we took one of its carry out menus just in case we are back this way in the future.

Looking down into the cutting from Myreside Road we find a class 60, 60 054 *Charles Babbage* on 6E30 the Dalzell to Tees steel empties. As you may imagine from the foliage overhanging the railway, this piece of line, which is also on an incline up to the summit at Morningside Road, can be very treacherous. The class 60 will not have such problems with this train. The signal for Craiglockhart junction can be seen just as the line curves out of view. Straight on takes you to Gorgie but if you get a colour and a 'feather' (the line of white lights indicating you are signalled to take the diverging line) you head for Slateford. I have been over this line with *Scots Guardsman* and the engine's bark may well have woken some of the residents of the nearby cemetery! Morningside Road Signal box's Up line distant, signal 13, was in this cutting over 900 yards from the box.

Looking west from the Cluny Avenue over bridge shows the stretch of line that the class 24 expired on requiring the Fire Brigade to attend. On this occasion however there was no drama for a class 60 in Colas livery which has just began to coast downhill for Blackford Hill and Newington. This is an empty cement from Inverness to Oxwellmains. I know this as I had been out to Gleneagles to see the train there earlier in the day. Colas are still in charge of the workings from Oxwellmains but now use class 70s. Class 60s, which used to be a daily sight on these metals, are no longer rostered for any duties round the Sub, or indeed into Scotland.

CHAPTER 5
MILLERHILL

The yard at Millerhill was still relatively busy in the early 1970s but even then not working at its intended capacity. The amount of traffic steadily declined, the yard shrank and the depot closed. Today there is through traffic, permanent way and engineer's sidings and a newly constructed depot for ScotRail electric units. My first visits to Millerhill were by bus, a number 14 whose terminus was beside the lines but about half a mile from the entrance to the depot and yard. You passed a level crossing and a couple of NCB steam locos at Niddrie Colliery. There was still a coal bing (spoil heap) on the other side of the road from the bus terminus. Looking from the road over bridge at the access road at the north end of the yard towards the bus terminus, you saw six lines and a relic of the steam age a water tower, either side of the railway was open ground. Today you will only see three lines, two for Millerhill and the third is the Borders railway. There is a dual carriageway, behind that Newcraighall Station and beyond, where the pit bing was, Fort Kinnaird Shopping Centre. Looking south, you saw the office block, the shed and opening out before you a large and at times busy yard with, on weekdays, two or more 08s going about their shunting. The yard had a control tower and the towers of Monktonhall colliery were on the skyline. The view today is very different.

Visiting on a weekday wouldn't show many locos on shed so a Saturday or better still Sunday afternoon was the best time to go as all the weekend engineering work had concluded and the locos were on shed and there were a lot! Getting round was never a problem; the usual problem was finding someone from whom to ask permission. As well as the 08s, usually at the fuel tanks, there were all the local 20s,24s, 25s, 26s and 27s. You would also find 37s, 40s, sometimes a 45 or 46 and 47s. It was amongst these classes that most of the 'cops' would come as the locos were from inter-regional freights. Class 31s were rare visitors here, and indeed elsewhere in the city, as neither the Millerhill or Haymarket crews signed them so if one did appear (I recall on a visit to Haymarket that the gaffer was on the telephone advising whoever was on the other end of the phone that he didn't know what ' a Brush 2' was and had no intention of receiving one on his shed) the loco would have to be worked back by the Gateshead or Tyne Yard men. The yard was also used for storing redundant locos so at various points there were lines of Claytons and Type 2s. There was also a single unit railcar which I recall was in use as a bothy.

Later on, class 56s began to appear on mainly coal trains, of which there were many. Electrification reached Millerhill on the through roads and now for the ScotRail facility. EWS took over the site and the ubiquitous class 66s were the staple traction; however, 37s were still in use, often on the Powderhall to Oxwellmains bin liner and class 60s could also be found on occasion as could 67s.

The yard was linked at the south to the Waverley route until its closure and to the ECML which allowed freights to enter the yard, perhaps have a crew change, and then carry on via the Sub thus avoiding Waverley. The shed hosted four class 60s for the remodelling of Waverley in the early 1990s. But as traffic reduced, the work for Millerhill men reduced significantly and the depot closed.

An observer at the same overbridge today would see trains for the Borders railway and electric units going to and from the ScotRail depot as well as freights such as cement from Oxwellmains (just south of Dunbar) for Aberdeen, Inverness or Uddingston, along with the GBRF Alcans for Fort William, DRS hauled flask trains to and from Torness, intermodal services for Grangemouth and Elderslie (near Paisley) and engineer's trains, the latter especially on Fridays and weekends.

Summer of 1973 and a very rare visitor to Edinburgh was eventually captured at Millerhill on a Sunday afternoon. 1663 *Sir Daniel Gooch* had appeared in Waverley on the Saturday morning but before I had arrived. It took two visits to Millerhill to find it, first time it was out on engineering work but second time round it was stabled on the shed and I suspect that it was not used to being in the company of class 26s and 27s. This was my first named Brush 4, in those days there were only seventeen named 47s and all were allocated to Western Region sheds. I don't think we ever found out what had brought this loco so far from home.

The early 1970s view from the road over bridge at the entrance to Millerhill shed and yard looking north. A class 20 on an engineer's working is coming into the yard. There are multiple running lines and a water tower, a remnant of the steam age. To the left of the floodlights was a coal bing and further west Niddrie Colliery and at this time there was still a road crossing and a couple of steam locos. The number 14 bus terminus was just across the road from the white building just at the foot of the floodlights. You can still stand at this observation point but the colliery and surrounds are now Fort Kinnaird retail Park, Newcraighall Fire Station has been built as has Newcraighall Station and park and ride car park however the view is obscured by a dual carriageway extension of the A1 trunk road.

We have crossed the road and are now looking across Millerhill yard, the office block roof is just visible behind the bushes to the left. There is plenty going on with two class 08s working the yard, a class 37 on a tank train which I suspect is oil and in the foreground a class 40, no doubt a Midland loco running round 4M45 which has come in from Bathgate and will now head for Carlisle via the Sub and Slateford on weekdays and Waverley on a Saturday. It is clear that even at this time part of the yard was already out of use. The headgear etc of Monktonhall Colliery is also seen.

We have moved along the road to look towards the office block and shed. As there are no 08s visible on the shed and only a couple of locos this must have been a weekday. The train entering the yard is unusual as the pair of class 20s are both bonnet leading as opposed to the more usual bonnet to bonnet pairing. Visibility from a 20s cab along the bonnet isn't good and the second man would be needed for sighting signals and general observation. The train too is unusual given that neither of the wagons visible would ordinarily require a brake van so I think these wagons must have been heading for the wagon repair facility that was at the bottom end of the yard. Again, you can stand on this spot today but the view is very different. The Borders line heads off to the right, the offices and shed are gone and only two lines remain and of course there is now OLE too. The ScotRail EMU depot now occupies some of the ground at the bottom of the yard roughly between the train of tanks and the shed although so much vegetation has grown up you can't actually see it.

Stabled on the shed roads are a 40 and a Peak awaiting their next duties. The control tower is seen here and what used to be an everyday sight, a yellow BR van. Peaks were not frequent visitors here, but they did turn up from time to time and I discovered that there was a Nottingham to Portobello freightliner which passed our house in the wee small hours which would be a Peak or a 47. 4G72 the Gushetfaulds to Portobello liner was also sometimes a Peak but that engine went light straight back to Glasgow after depositing its train at Portobello.

It is 1985 and considerable work has been ongoing to clear away the now unused running lines and water tower and construction of the A1 extension is underway. There is an unusual combination of a class 37 and class 20. Newcraighall Station will be built at the other side of the A1 bridge we can see but not for several years yet.

A March 1985 image catches a class 37 just outside the small shed at Millerhill. As the back roads have no locos stabled, I suspect that this was a weekday visit. The 37 still carries rail blue, as almost everything was when my interest in railways began (apart from the odd green loco) but the head-code box has been plated over. It is interesting that those same head-codes are still used for the train description code for working timetables and for inputting to GSM-R. I am told that the fitter at Millerhill was quite adept at doing brake block changes so perhaps this 37 has just had that work carried out.

In the same year, we see a classic Sunday afternoon line up at Millerhill. These are the two roads at the back of the shed. The 08s were usually stabled by the fuelling point, sometimes there would be a loco in the head shunt and there was a road on the other side of the shed which would also be full of locos and as I recall that road would tend to have the type 3 and 4s whereas the back roads would tend to have the type 2s, although there is a 47 in this picture. Of course, none of the locos would be 'cops' for me but I can imagine what an enthusiast from say the West Midlands would have made of this sight.

The water tower and several of the running lines have gone. The A1 dual carriageway extension has been built but Newcraighall station has not. Quite a change from the earlier views. An everyday sight of a pair of class 20s on box wagons. The various sources of instant information available to today's enthusiasts, such as 'freightmaster' and 'real time trains' were not available to us, so I have no idea what this working was. The only way to glean such information was to get hold of a working timetable. We didn't have mobile phones either, so if there was something unusual on the go it was often gone before you became aware of it.

The same train from the other side of the road bridge and this demonstrates how the yard is already significantly reduced in size. The office block can be seen to the left of the picture, on a Sunday afternoon it would be deserted. The shed still seems to have a fair number of locos stabled there. The sidings cannot be all that long gone as the vegetation has not taken hold as it eventually will. Millerhill was a useful source of assistance for failures; nowadays, there is no such resource and, as I write these captions, today and yesterday a freightliner and the loaded steel have slipped to a stand on the Sub and assistance has taken several hours to appear, possibly from Mossend.

A typical working for a Haymarket 26 would be a mixed freight of this type. It is about to enter Millerhill. Grainflow wagons were quite a common sight in the area with rail linked sites for loading grain still existing and delivery may well be to the brewing or distilling industries which again still had some rail connections. It is correct to say that I would see class 26s every weekday passing by the house.

The days of rail blue were numbered as sector liveries started to appear. This 37 displays railfreight livery of grey plus red stripe along the bottom of the bodyside. This looks like an engineer's working. Whilst freight of different types still passes through Millerhill, engineer's trains still find the yard as a destination although today they are most likely to be hauled by a class 66.

We can see just how few lines there are left in this picture of an Eastfield allocated (the West Highland Terrier emblem gives the allocation away) 37 on fuel tanks. There had just been a crew change for this freight. The shed is still in use and classes 47, 37 and 20 are seen. Much of the yard has however gone. The vegetation hasn't established itself just yet so the rails cannot have been lifted for that long. It does show just how marked the contraction of the yard was.

A class 26 has been refurbished, note the plated over connecting doors and the head-code discs have been removed giving a much less cluttered looking front. It is sporting the same railfreight livery as the 37 and works a very typical of the day short and probably local service. This is an interesting picture for a modern image modeller. Even in O gauge this would be a manageable train to recreate.

The A1 extension is up and running as are the OLE wires, we can see too that the line side vegetation has begun to take hold. This is a class of loco that I do not have many pictures of, in Scotland at least, as by the time they had started to appear in the Edinburgh area I was elsewhere. But here we have a class 56 with coal sector branding working a coal train, of which there were many. Class 56s are certainly distinctive in appearance and sound, especially when working hard. Just now and again I still see a 56 on engineer's workings in Colas livery. The Grangemouth to Prestwick aviation fuel tankers used to be a common job for a 56.

Into the EWS era and the signage at the gate at the north end of the yard where the drive to the offices and shed leave the main road. Engineer's trains still use Millerhill and it has been used as a virtual quarry; however, the locomotives used come from different operators and not just DB as EWS became. Weekend engineering operations now often produce either light engine moves or double or triple heading of trains to move locos to Millerhill for the weekend.

An image from 2003, the dual carriageway blocks the view and Newcraighall Station is just at the other side of the road over bridge. Only two running lines remain and the third line is a head shunt to allow ScotRail services terminating at Newcraighall to move out of the way before forming their next train. This spur would become the Borders line in due course, the original Waverley route was at the south end of Millerhill. The train is a very typical working of its day, the ubiquitous class 66 on loaded MGR wagons. I am afraid I cannot say where the train had come from or was heading to. For once I seem to have taken an image of the everyday workings.

The shed is still active in this 2001 view which shows a ScotRail class 158 unit in the head shunt between services. The yard is wired and 90 035 is on one of the North Berwick sets with a DVT on the other end. I am not at all sure why it was at Millerhill. It is possible to come off the ECML at Monktonhall Junction and through Millerhill to get to Waverley rejoining the main line at Portobello. An EWS driver would certainly know the road to do this, but I am told that very few LNER drivers sign the road through Millerhill and onto the ECML via Monktonhall Junction which would be, to my mind anyway, a useful diversion to know. The shed is host to a 66.

66 113 has charge of a mixed freight; it became unusual to see different types of wagons in trains. I suspect this is the 'alcan' working for Fort William. There is a 37 on the shed head shunt and no doubt that would be used on the bins that day. There doesn't appear to be anything else on shed so perhaps the run down of Millerhill as a depot is already underway. EWS had hoped to secure work for Royal Mail but when that fell through the amount of work for crews based at Millerhill was so small that it ceased to be a depot.

The trees and bushes are taking over! The Borders railway still isn't open. There was nothing much to be seen on the shed or in the yard as I recall except for a Class 47 on the 'Royal Scotsman' charter train. This has become a very popular tourist attraction and now has its own specially liveried class 66s as traction. The Royal Scotsman still visits Edinburgh, and it can be seen on the Sub from time to time. If memory serves me correctly, the 47 has also had a livery for this train applied. Millerhill is used for running round trains or turning them using Niddire West Junction so that may well be what is happening here.

The location is Newcraighall Station and 66 605 has a cement train no doubt empty and bound for Oxwellmains; as this was mid-afternoon, I suspect it had come from Uddingston. This is another view that you could not repeat today as Colas took over the cement workings and the same train today would be class 70 hauled and possibly with different wagons too. This freight was a bonus as I had gone out to Newcraighall for the steel empties. The bins and the steel were favourite workings for Edinburgh based enthusiasts and photographers.

Not long after the cement in the previous photograph had appeared, a ScotRail 158 turned up followed shortly by the working I had been waiting for, 60 062 in its EWS livery on the steel empties. As the working started from just this side of Motherwell, it tended to turn up at its booked time. I confess to having a liking for these machines. They look the part and the two-tone grey and this livery suited them well. The sound of a 60 working hard, such as on the loaded steel, is also quite impressive. As I recall I was not the only photographer at Newcraighall that afternoon.

If the processor's date stamp is correct, this image is from September 2016. The picture is taken from a new road which takes you onto what was the original yard but now has two industrial plants, one of which is an incinerator. The road goes over the Borders line and then runs parallel with the Millerhill through lines which are in the foreground. The building, clearly out of use, is Millerhill shed, a place I must have visited many times over the years. The yard control tower has already gone. I decided to drive out and take a photo of the shed. I have always thought that Millerhill shed would make a very good subject for an MPD model railway which could be flexible about the era you wished to model. As it turned out, I was very glad that I had ventured out and taken this picture as two days later the shed was demolished.

CHAPTER 6
EAST COAST MAIN LINE

Edinburgh is of course an integral and, for most services, a terminating destination on the ECML. In the early and mid-1970s, Deltics and 47s were the mainstay traction. Of course, because these were everyday sights, I tended not to photograph them. One working that occasionally provided a 45 or 46 was the 10:06 Plymouth. Deltics and 47s gave way to HSTs and I can recall the prototype HST visiting the city. In time, the HSTs were superseded by class 91 electrics and they too have now been replaced with Hitachi electric and bi mode units.

The only commuter services I can recall are those to North Berwick, the other branch lines, to Musselburgh, Macmerry, Gifford, Gullane and Haddington, had closed by my time. Over the years, the citizens of that town have had quite a variety of traction working their trains, from DMUs, through 150 units, Class 90 and DVT sets to a variety of different EMUs.

Cockenzie Power Station was served by 'merry go round' trains usually class 26 hauled. The same class were the staple power for trains from Blindwells too, but both of these facilities are long closed and demolished. Torness nuclear plant is still generating electricity and flasks come and go by rail. The principal freight centre remains the cement works at Oxwellmains, just south of Dunbar, which has services both north and southbound. A unique feature used to be that the industrial shunters there were capable of working onto the main line as the site's wagon repair facility was on the other side of the ECML from the plant itself. It was also the destination for bin liner trains from Powderhall in Edinburgh and similar workings from Manchester. The bin liners were emptied on the north side of the main line. The failure of the compactor at Powderhall put a stop to the bin liner trains from Edinburgh.

Prestonpans was always a favourite spot as in the car park you were at rail level and there was quite a wide view with the lines for Cockenzie Power Station. The old Haddington branch trackbed is also an interesting vantage point and is accessed from Longniddry Station. Over the years, new stations were built at Musselburgh and Wallyford with plans for further stations at Reston and East Linton.

The Freedom of Scotland rover ticket only took you as far as Berwick upon Tweed, where, as you will see, could be found the most northerly working for a class 03 shunter.

Of course, with electrification came many changes but that did ensure that HSTs continued in use on the London to Aberdeen and Inverness services and it is only relatively recently that bi mode LNER Hitachi units have taken over those services. Electrification makes photography more difficult and some of the spots I used are no longer viable.

It is to my regret that I do not have many photos of Deltics going about their everyday work on ECML express passenger trains. It was such a common sight that we didn't stop to think and record them. The same goes for class 27s on the Edinburgh to Glasgow push pulls. Here is one of the few I do have, taken with a Kodak Instamatic as the Deltics had gone by the time I could afford an SLR. This is Drem junction and the branch line is that for North Berwick. An unidentified class 55 heads south. I never saw a Deltic in two tone green, my last one was *Alycidon,* which I copped at Haymarket one Saturday afternoon when it was in the running shed and instantly recognisable as it was the first to receive the domino head-code.

I think this was the furthest north Class 03 shunters ever came. When I bought my first *British Railways Locomotives and Other Motive Power Combined Volume* (Ian Allan), shunters in Scotland were either 08s or Andrew Barclay 06s. It is stabled in Berwick upon Tweed station and was used to work the yards at the other side of the Border Bridge. This picture was taken from the train I was travelling south on. The 03 was allocated to Gateshead and swapping the engines over must have been a very long and stop start job for the crew. Today of course the need for shunting locomotives has reduced considerably so scenes like this do not appear very often. More is the pity to my mind.

Prestonpans station looking south. The wires are up but the fencing that adorns the railway hasn't yet been built. Given the quality of the light, this is an evening shot. I am not aware what the working is. I had gone out 'on spec' as it was a nice evening. The freight will be heading to Millerhill. The 47, still in rail blue, has a very distinct cant rail and a light grey roof, another of the seemingly endless variations of livery on these numerous locos. The blue has seen better days so perhaps a repaint was overdue.

An HST in the later Inter City livery speeds north for Edinburgh. This is Longniddry station, and the track bed of the Haddington Branch can be seen to the right of the running lines. This is a walkway/cycle path but as Haddington expands as a town I wonder if the branch line might make a comeback one day. The yellow stripe is evident on the platforms and as trains do pass through this station at speed, an indicator of the minimum safe distance is required.

Once the HSTs had taken over the principal ECML services, the secondary or additional trains were almost all hauled by the ubiquitous class 47s. A member of the class heads south on a rather 'dreich' day. No wires are evident yet and the footbridge is in original condition. With the coming of electrification, the footbridges at the various stations had to be rebuilt to accommodate the overhead line equipment. One of the footbridges from an East Lothian station found its way to Prestongrange but alas it has never been rebuilt.

The North Berwick branch has seen very many different types of rolling stock over the years and here is another example. The location is Longniddry and this two car class 150 unit will be working between North Berwick and Edinburgh for most of the day. The first signs of OLE construction are apparent so it will not be too long before the North Berwicks turn over to electric traction.

The location is East Linton and this was a special working to mark the last days of the Class 27s. As I recall it was destined for York and return but at least one of the pair of 27s didn't last out the day. This is one of the towns that is to be reconnected to the rail network with the building of a new station. Whilst the weather that day wasn't good, I couldn't pass up the chance to record what might be the last 27 passenger working I might see. A pity I had not thought to record them when they were an everyday sight!

In August of 1988 I heard that a class 26 had come to grief at catch-points on one of the loops at Grantshouse. We set off down the A1 to see what had happened, but I did not expect to find this sight. 26 029 had not only derailed but had also toppled over. Recovery of the loco took some time. Electrification work is ongoing but HSTs are still the frontline traction. We were able to walk right up to the stricken loco; no doubt today the site would be cordoned off and spectators would not be welcome.

It is 2001 and the electrification is complete, including the North Berwick branch. This view at Drem shows yet another different type of unit for the branch trains. As was often the case, the sets in use were cascades from elsewhere, in this case the Eastern Region. As well as the junction, there are loops either side of the main line just east of Drem station. These are often used for steam charters and freights; the Oxwellmains to Powderhall binliner could often be found here waiting its path amongst the frequent passenger services of various operators.

Once more in East Lothian, we encounter an unusual sight for those days – a double headed freight, two class 47s in contrasting liveries. These are ammonia tanks and would be bound for Tees Yard. It is complete with a brake van and a barrier wagon. The train will have come from Leith (we saw a 47/3 at Seafield with a similar working earlier). Whilst the wires are up and live, freight was very much still diesel hauled.

Located just to the East of Prestonpans was Blindwells. This was an open cast coal mine and had a loading facility for merry go round trains comprised of the familiar HAA or HBA wagons. Several of the local class 26 fleet were fitted for 'MGR' workings and this is just such a working. The class 26 has been refurbished and turned out in large logo railfreight livery but may well have gone on to receive the coal sector livery. This mining operation has closed and the site cleared so that a development of some 1,600 houses could be built. Today you would be hard pressed to realise that this industrial site had existed.

Another evening freight at Prestonpans, this time a class 37 in railfreight livery. Again, I would not have known what the wagons contained (I have a suspicion it may have been loose sand or fertilizer) but whatever it is there is a considerable dust cloud rising from the wagons. This will inevitably be destined in the first instance for Millerhill. Open wagons were still an everyday sight on the railways then but like so many aspects of the stock and infrastructure that I was familiar with are now long gone.

We are at Prestonpans again, the wires are up but the fencing that seems to follow electrification has not been erected so there is still a good ground level view. It is August 2003 according to the date stamp on the photograph and I was fortunate (I assume the passengers onboard this no doubt delayed service did not have the same outlook) to catch a class 67 'Thunderbird' doing a rescue job on a GNER class 91 and train. The 67 was stabled either at Waverley or Craigentinny and crewed by a GNER driver. Sometimes it would venture out round the Sub or up to Millerhill, but only as far as the yard entry from Newcraighall as the GNER drivers did not sign through the yard. They were also used to drag HST power cars to and from Craigentinny. It was very useful to have a rescue loco around but with the departure of HSTs and 91s, they went too. I do have to wonder, however, if one of the Hitachi units slipped to a stand on the Sub, just how would it get rescued? I must say that I can only recall seeing a 67 in action as a 'Thunderbird' two or three times. It is amusing that such a high tech loco as a 67 has a very large brass key that needs to be used in the start-up process.

Another GNER class 91 set, this time photographed from the old Haddington branch which is now a walkway/cycle path from Longniddry to Haddington. This was a favourite location as you get some exercise and a full view of the train. The dark blue livery was quite impressive and the crests on the coaches, which now change hands for not insignificant amounts of cash, added a touch of class. This image is from 2006 and we can also see that crops are growing and being protected by an automated bird scaring device.

We are further south, within sight of Torness power Station, which has its own railhead for DRS to remove and deliver nuclear flasks, traffic which still runs with Class 68s but for a long time was the preserve of DRS 37s. The 91 set is still in the GNER livery with the red line along the side, when GNER's parent company failed the new operator replaced the red line with white. I recall this trip out as I had come across a large telephoto lens second hand in a local camera shop and it had the correct fitting so that I could use it with my Fujica camera. I also had to buy a tripod as it was impossible to hold the lens so I went out to see what was going on and try a few test shots and this is one of those.

Another view from 2006 at East Linton, the A1 is now dual carriageway at this point so this photo was taken from the old main road and shows an impressive field of oil seed rape just turning that distinctive yellow and quite a common crop in East Lothian. Interestingly, East Linton is one of the towns on the ECML that has had plans for a new station approved so this view will change in the not too distant future. I suspect that I had begged my boss for a half day on flexi-time to be able to get out and about to catch the empty steel which left Millerhill about 15:20. I will have seen that there was a 60, with metals sector livery on the steel in the morning as the steel often went through Newington on the Sub just as I was walking to work. So here we have a metals sector loco working a metals sector train.

A winter's morning at Prestonpans station in 2004. As I recall, these class 322 units had been cascaded and were now working the North Berwick trains and this example has not received a livery change to ScotRail colours. The North Berwick trains certainly saw variety in terms of classes of units used and of course the 90s and DVT sets. It is interesting to note the yellow line on the platform which is there to keep passengers the correct distance from the tracks as trains pass through the station nonstop. There are also automated warnings messaged from the tannoy system advising those on the platforms of approaching trains. As the distance looks like 2 metres, the speed limit at Prestonpans will be in excess of 100mph. The population of this town has grown considerably since this picture was taken and the North Berwick services are well used by commuters.

It is the same Saturday morning and I confess that I had not gone to Prestonpans to photograph EMUs. The station provides a good view of approaching traffic in both directions but to the south the lines are straight and traffic can be seen from some way off. I had ventured out to see if there was a class 37 on the Oxwellmains to Powderhall empty bin liner and looking down the lines to the south I was able to see, and of course hear, that there was indeed a 37 on the job. 37 419 is in charge on this occasion. Originally D6991, it entered service in 1965 in South Wales. It is quite a testament to these locomotives that there are still examples in active service today and indeed from time to time I hear them passing by on the Sub!

Another view of Prestonpans and again a service bound for North Berwick. However, instead of a unit this is another example of the class90 and DVT sets that were used. The date on the photograph is 2005. The class 90 is in almost GNER livery and I think this was unique to this engine which, to confuse railway enthusiasts, does not appear to be displaying a tops number. I wonder if those using the service had a preference out of the varied rolling stock used. A friend of mine who drives for ScotRail had been on the North Berwicks and described to me a gentleman wearing a judicial-looking suit who had been taking an interest in what he, the driver, was doing. I instantly recognised who it was and told my friend so next time he saw the same gent he said, 'Good morning, Sheriff Scott'. A couple of days later I was in Sheriff Scott's company and asked if his train driver had greeted him recently and he replied with some surprise that had indeed happened. He was amused when I explained how the greeting had come about.

We are just east of Prestonpans and on the other side of the line from where Blindwells was and amazingly the usual fencing hasn't been erected so it was possible to obtain a decent 'under the wires' view of Deltic 19 *Royal Highland Fusilier*, heading to Edinburgh on a rail-tour in 2005. It is good to see a Deltic back on its original home turf. Number 19 turned up at one of the NYMR diesel galas that I have worked at, so I have had a wee drive of the machine. Not the easiest to drive, especially for tasks such as buffering up as you go from no amps to very many amps in an instant. Happily, my driver that day, the excellent Gerry Skelton, was an ex-York man so he knew just how to control our steed!

It is 2006 and we are back on the Haddington branch; in the background and across the Forth is the Kingdom of Fife and a freighter is on the river heading most likely for Grangemouth, although shipping still uses Leith and Rosyth. The steel empties are being hauled by 60 046 *William Wilberforce*. By this time, EWS had decided to show their ownership of these locos by covering their sector branding with their 'three beasties' stickers and the yellow and red doesn't quite go with the two tone grey the way the sector decals did. The steel was originally a re-man at Millerhill, but that changed over the years. When it runs now it is a 66 duty; the 66 has a better top speed. However, for going round the Sub with the loaded train, the hauling power of a 60 might be more suitable.

Another bread and butter freight was the movement of coal for power generation, steel making and other industrial processes. On privatisation, EWS had the monopoly of such services before Freightliner moved into the market. So this was an everyday sight of a 66, in this case 66 047, on a lengthy rake of HAAs, or members of that family of wagons, bound I suspect for Tyne Yard. This picture was taken on the same day as the previous image, and it was quite unusual for me to record workings like this. I am glad I did, as it wasn't too long before the wagons used for such flows changed to a more modern design and of course coal trains now are very much a rarity.

We are further east now and another 66 on another coal train. However, 66 117 is heading north with newer wagons with a much greater capacity. Again, I am not at all sure where this load would be heading; it would most likely have originated at Tyne Yard. It would have been unusual for me to record such a workaday train but perhaps I was conscious that the wagons were different and should be recorded, I suspect however that I was out and about for something else and took the opportunity to shoot the coal train.

Another 322 unit but this one has acquired its First Group ScotRail livery. It is heading to Edinburgh Waverley having just left the North Berwick branch at Drem Junction and is passing between the Drem loops and will shortly call at Drem station. The telephoto lens has been employed here. Whilst the North Berwick branch survives today the other East Lothian branch lines to Musselburgh, Macmerry, Gifford, Haddington and Gullane are all no more. The class 322 units are gone too, as has the First Group livery.

The other mainstay of East Coast services were the HSTs. I can recall the prototype visiting Waverley and gradually the production sets began to appear and the Deltics' days were numbered. The HSTs were essential for the Aberdeen and Inverness trains even after electrification to Waverley. Some of the ECML Aberdeens are worked by an Edinburgh crew but others and the Inverness by a Newcastle crew. These services are now in the hands of bi-mode Hitachi units although ScotRail now operate HSTs in shortened formats on the Edinburgh and Glasgow to Inverness and Aberdeen routes. This HST set is in the 'East Coast' branded livery and is seen just west of Drem.

As I have suggested, the steel and the bins were popular freight workings for photographers, the steel for class 60s and the bins for the variety of traction involved in that working and especially the 37s. I had intended to catch this working at Drem as it was often looped to allow faster trains to pass, given the class 60s speed limitation, but it was already away from there so was lucky that there was a lay-by free so I could stop and catch this image of 60 092 *Reginald Munns,* complete with EWS sticker. The shot shows the equipment behind the front grille to good effect. The bins no longer run and two tone grey 60s in traffic are a memory now too.

CHAPTER 7

DALMENY & FIFE

Dalmeny is of course the station on the south end of the Forth Rail Bridge. It is also a junction with the lines from the west (via Winchburgh Junction) joining those from Edinburgh and there remains a public footpath at track level which gives a fine view of the passing traffic. The path was the trackbed of the line to South Queensferry. There are also sidings and the base for bridge operations. Interestingly, the lines at Dalmeny Station are bi directional.

Dalmeny Station is quite a good spot to photograph specials using the bridge and recently that has been SRPS steam hauled circle tours and 'The Aberdonian' charters pulled by *Tornado*. I have had the good fortune to have crossed the bridge on the footplate in each direction, northbound on Jubilee *Galatea* just as the sun was coming up and south on 46115 *Scots Guardsman*. The climb from Inverkeithing up through Ferry Road and North Queensferry Tunnels is profound and the Scot was working hard throughout. Certainly, in steam days banking was the order of the day here. The Western seen earlier struggled and I heard that it left its mark on the railheads such was the severity of its slipping.

North Queensferry is the station at the north end of the bridge. From there the line descends to Inverkeithing and thereafter trains can head either for Burntisland or Dunfermline. It used to be possible to climb up the hill and look down on Jamestown Viaduct (and Wards scrapyard which had an industrial diesel) but in modern times fencing has put a stop to that. As there is a water treatment plant nearby it wasn't a very pleasant place to spend too long! There is also a link to Rosyth from Inverkeithing.

The line to Kirkcaldy still had steam at the Burntisland aluminium plant. Seafield Colliery was still open as was the tightly curved and steeply graded Kirkcaldy harbour branch. Also still in use was the branch to the Frances pit. I think it was Dunfermline that provided the Barclay 06 for Kirkcaldy and another engine of the same class could be found at Markinch for the paper mill branch. Markinch was also the home for Sir John Cameron's *Union of South Africa* for some years. I never managed to get to Dunfermline Townhill shed and by the time I visited Thornton it was a very pale shadow of the yard it once had been and was in use for storing withdrawn locos. More recently we had an overnight stop there with *Scots Guardsman* returning from Perth after hauling a Ryder Cup charter from Waverley to Gleneagles. Thornton's contraction was similar to Millerhill's. On the bright side, in Fife work is ongoing to reinstate the Leven branch to carry passengers once more.

My recollection of Fife bound trains was mostly DMUs with loco haulage if the train was going beyond Dundee or, via Newburgh to Perth. For a while the Dundees were class 27 hauled. The Aberdeens were usually 40s or 47s. In later years, travelling to Aberdeen for university 158s had arrived. Of course, loco-hauled services were revived for Fife commuter trains morning and night latterly DRS 68s and Mk2 stock. However, that entailed empty stock workings to and from the Motherwell area twice a day. Right up to date, ScotRail HST sets do the honours, for the traveller surely a vast improvement on 158 or 170 units.

This is Inverkeithing Central Junction, the class 47, complete with snow ploughs will be on an Aberdeen to Edinburgh working and the coaching stock has a restaurant car and at least two of the coaches are in 'Inter City' livery. The 47 has come off the Kirkcaldy line, the left hand lines go to Dunfermline then Cowdenbeath and Cardenden, through Thornton completing the "Fife Circle" at the various Thornton Junctions. After the Edinburgh to Glasgows went over to 47/7s and a DBSO some of the Glasgow and Edinburgh to Aberdeen services also use that type of formation. I don't have many pictures of large logo 47s it turns out.

The same location and the same day but this time a class 27 and this will have been a Dundee to Edinburgh working as these were, for a while, almost always a 27 job. I don't recall why this wasn't a DMU turn, but the enthusiasts of the day, particularly the haulage men, were not complaining. Haulage was something that never appealed to me but I can understand the attraction, especially if your favourite class had a distinctive sound to them. I overheard a couple of haulage men at NYMR after they had enjoyed a run from Pickering to Grosmont behind a class 45 and described the sounds of the peak hard at work as 'symphonic'! The driver had deliberately slowed before applying a lot of power for the stiff climb up to Newtondale Halt where, as always on diesel galas, there was someone wanting to get on thus providing a restart on the gradient away from the Halt and more Sulzer 'music'. I smiled to myself as it had been my hand on the power controller; well, you should give the public what they want sometimes!

Another class 27, this time heading for Dundee. There seem to be plenty of passengers about at this station stop. I have a suspicion that the 27s' work on this job was coming to an end, so I had gone out to record the scene before they were replaced. A run round the Fife coast at this time would be quite interesting as the aluminium plant at Burntisland with its industrial steam was still very much in production as was Seafield Colliery and there was still a yard at Kirkcaldy Station with the prospect of seeing Andrew Barclay 06 shunters too.

A Metro Cammell three car unit powers away from Dalmeny having just crossed the Forth Bridge from Fife. This shows the layout of the tracks well and shows the engineer's sidings where a track machine is stabled. This is an absolutely typical working of its day. I have done one shift on a similar unit at North Yorkshire, and they are powerful and quite sprightly.

I think this was taken on the same day. It was quite unusual for me to photograph units but here in Dalmeny station are another Metro Cammell (they really were the most common units in the area) this time heading for Fife as evidenced by the white lights to the front and a Swindon unit heading for Edinburgh, sporting red lights. It must be remembered that these lines are bi-directional. When I started going to Waverley and underlining numbers the only Swindon built units in Scotland were those based at Ayr and those used on the Aberdeen to Inverness route and they did not appear in Edinburgh. Swindon units were cascaded from Central Wales and Derby.

An evening trip to South Queensferry allowed me to take this image of the approaches to the main sections of the Forth Rail Bridge. Of course, the train just had to be a three car Metro Cammell set; sometimes we did wonder if there were any other sorts of units. There were a few Cravens and I recall a Gloucester unit still in green livery on the go. Network Rail are working on a visitor centre for the bridge.

Happily I discovered amongst my photographs that I had managed to record some class 27s at work. While the Dundees were in the hands of 27s there was an opportunity to catch them. This one is at Dalmeny Junction with the line from Winchburgh visible. This is a busy location as can be seen by the rear of a multiple unit just visible under the road bridge. At the left side of the tracks there is now a fence and a pathway which includes use of the track-bed of the line down to South Queensferry.

Taken from the same bridge but looking towards Dalmeny station again a class 47 heads for Edinburgh. To my mind this is too short a rake for an Aberdeen service so it may have come from Dundee or Perth via Newburgh and Ladybank. I suppose with 508 examples to choose from, it was no surprise that class 47s appeared so often and at so many locations. A blue 47 on Mk I stock; an everyday sight for enthusiasts of my vintage but a piece of history for those of today.

We have crossed the Forth into Fife and are looking down on Jamestown Viaduct. Again this is a location you can no longer access as a fence has been erected halfway up the hillside. It wasn't the most pleasant place to be as there is a water treatment plant nearby. The line for Rosyth passes underneath. To the right is Wards scrapyard which had its own industrial shunter in those days. Whilst it was mostly a ship breaking yard, some rolling stock was scrapped there. Another class 47 is in charge of four Mk 1s.

No visit to Fife would be complete without an image from Muir's. This scrapyard was famous for holding a collection of ex NCB and Wemyss Railway industrial steam engines and I have heard it described as 'the Barry of the North'. It certainly was not as vast as Woodham's and as well as the steam engines had a wide variety of scrap which gradually engulfed the locomotives. As well as the usual cars and so on I recall there being an ancient open cab turntable ladder fire engine and a small submarine in the yard. This too is no more, and the remaining steam locos were moved to a yard adjacent to the railway in Kirkcaldy.

Coasting downhill towards Inverkeithing is another three car Metro Cammel unit in the later blue and white livery. These were all in rail blue in the early '70s. The climb from Inverkeithing up to North Queensferry is a steep one and in steam days banking of freights was common. The noise in the tunnels made by 46115 *Scots Guardsman* was deafening.

I see that the zoom lens is in use here as another of the Swindon's is seen again about to tackle the climb out of Inverkeithing. It is a real shame that this location isn't as accessible now. When this photo was taken there was a lot more variety of traffic on the go. Thornton Yard was still active, and coal was still a major aspect of rail freight. Loco hauled trains were still relatively common. I feel sorry for today's enthusiasts as units have taken over almost all passenger workings; however, I suppose there is more variety of unit types and liveries.

Back at Dalmeny we find an unusual combination of a 37 and 47. I suspect that the 47 is a failure and the 37 has been called upon to assist. Finding a loco to assist wasn't too great a problem as there were still depots and yards where locos could be found stabled and crews so delays resulting from loco failures could be controlled. Today, however, there are very few spare locos to be found. Recently, on two consecutive days, freight trains slipped to a stand on the Edinburgh Sub. The first, a class 66 on the loaded steel had to wait for over two hours for assistance to arrive and the second, a 66 on an intermodal, almost three hours. We speculated that Mossend might be the closest place to find an available 'thunderbird'.

One livery that I always thought suited the class 47s very well was the ScotRail one. This example is seen tackling the climb to North Queensferry. This will be from Aberdeen, but the loco isn't paired with one of the push pull sets which also carried the ScotRail livery, instead it has a mixture of Inter City and blue and white Mk 2 stock. The 47 shouldn't have any problems with the climb, unlike the class 52 Western.

This class 47 on freight was a bonus. I had gone to North Queensferry to photograph 60532 *Blue Peter* coming off the Forth Bridge and whilst waiting 47 287 appeared. Again, I had no knowledge of what this working was or where it was headed to, but it made a welcome change from DMUs.

Time has moved on and the seemingly ever-present Metro Cammells have been replaced by the next generation of DMUs and that meant class 150s, like this example, class 156 and 158 and later 170s. The initial branding of 'sprinters' and 'super sprinters' did not inspire me. I haven't travelled on many 150s but did commute on 156s, 158s and 170s. As a personal preference I would prefer loco hauled coaching stock.

Also at North Queensferry an HST bound for Aberdeen, the Inverness HST was routed via Stirling to Perth, comes off the north end of the Rail bridge. There is little doubt that the HSTs were an excellent concept and design and have lasted the test of time. They are also considerably more comfortable, in my opinion, than newer Voyagers, Pendolinos or 803 units. They are once again in use on ScotRail services between Edinburgh and Glasgow to Inverness and Aberdeen and surely a great improvement for passengers.

The prospect of seeing a Deltic come off the Forth Bridge was too much of a temptation to resist, so here we have *Royal Highland Fusilier* returning to Edinburgh from Aberdeen on a rail-tour. As a lot of rail-tours went over the bridge, Dalmeny was a convenient spot to photograph them and the station has a large car park. The 'Aberdonian' title has been used again recently but this time with *Tornado* as a result of the Ferryhill turntable being brought back into use. The tour has mark 1 stock, possibly the SRPS rake and from memory this tour was very well patronised as the Deltics enjoy a cult following.

Dalmeny station again but this photo is interesting as it demonstrates that the running lines are bi-directional. Note that each line has a signal for proceeding north onto the bridge and compare this with the photo of the Deltic coming off the bridge which is using the other line. The class 170 unit must be a recent arrival as it has not yet received its ScotRail branding. The 170s were to become the mainstay of the longer distance services and the Edinburgh to Glasgow line. Having travelled a lot on 158s whilst commuting, the 170s were a vast improvement. I doubt however that our haulage friends would agree that any unit could be an improvement on loco-hauled trains. I do wonder if these units are comfortable enough or have sufficient capacity for longer haul trips such as that to Inverness, possibly why we now have shortened HST sets on such runs. The 170s were good units and one driver has described the experience as similar to driving in a bay window!

Below left: If the Deltic was worth going out to see then it was trumped by this tour, class 50s over the bridge. Now, 50s did appear from time to time when they worked the West Coast Main Line, but I had never seen one on the Forth Bridge. This particular tour was top and tailed with 50s for this run and had also gone round the Sub top and tailed. These are complex machines and, perhaps because they were a relatively small class and have a distinct sound, have their devotees. They have also operated in different parts of the country. From their early days as front line WCML, power prior to electrification, double heading Euston to Glasgow Central services, through a spell on the Western Region (obtaining former Warship class names) to their swansong with Network SouthEast. I have been in the engine room of one of these engines and it is compact! They also can rival their EE cousins the Deltics at creating a smoke screen on start up!

Below right: Another service coming off the bridge from Aberdeen this time a GNER era HST. This is a 2005 image and some sixteen years on, HSTs are still going to Aberdeen. This was an everyday scene, but this is the only photo I have of a GNER Aberdeen service. It is a lodging turn for the crews and, from my university days, having a liking for 'butteries' or 'rowies' (Aberdeen rolls which are more akin to pastry than bread) now and again my driver friend Ross would give me a call to tell me to be at platform 1 at a set time to collect a bag of rowies off his Aberdeen job. One evening the back of 21:00 I had gone to Waverley after just such a phone call. The HST came to a halt, the driver's cab door opened and a bag of rowies was handed over, almost at once the cab door was shut again as one yellow had come up on the signal and the set was away to Craigentinny. Walking back down the platform I was stopped by a couple of inquisitive BTP officers thinking that maybe I was up to something. The look on their faces when they saw the contents of the paper bag said it all!

CHAPTER 8
PERTHSHIRE & THE HIGHLANDS

I know this is a very large geographical area. My earliest trips north were to the West Highlands and in due course a mate and I used the Highland Travel Pass to tour the extremities of the rail system. This fine ticket allowed you on trains, boats and buses and as a result, by use of the ferries I made my only visits to Mull and Orkney and allowed us to go from Mallaig to Kyle of Lochalsh. The scenery is spectacular and the potential for 'trains in the landscape' pictures are many.

On my earliest trip, class 37s were in charge of passenger services but soon units, 156s which are still running today, had taken over. This was the same for the West Highland and the Far North lines to Wick and Thurso. In Perthshire, the Highland Main line had class 47s (which had taken over from the double headed 26s or a 24 and a 26) as the main traction. However, units took over there too and there was the HST from London for Inverness. Living in the central belt you really do forget just how far away Inverness actually is. My visits did allow me to record some long gone aspects of the railways such as Mallaig shed and the use of a Metro Cammell DMU as a form of observation car on the Kyle line. Whilst on Mull I am glad that I visited the now sadly closed railway there.

Moving to Perth in 1985 enabled me to investigate that area rather more fully. There was a rail fair in the yards which attracted interesting visitors including a Deltic and a Jubilee, which, as I recall, remained in the carriage shed at the station for some weeks after. I have had the pleasure of coming into Perth from the south on the footplate of *Scots Guardsman* from the Stirling line and *Galatea* via Newburgh. From the north, I was allowed, under the watchful eyes of our driver Peter Walker and fireman Pete Hanson, to fire *Galatea* from Pitlochry to Perth. I also had to commute for several years firstly to Dundee (usually by car) and latterly to Glasgow where I renewed my acquaintances with 158s. The Perthshire scenery, whilst not as rugged, is equally impressive as the West Highlands and the Highland main line runs through much of it. I was interested to see that part of the shed building at Blair Atholl still stands and on the same trip discovered that one of the nameplates from the early Warship diesel hydraulic *Sir Brian Robertson* is on display at the small museum at House of Bruar.

As elsewhere in Scotland, the railway system has contracted. Perth once boasted a very busy shed with a large allocation of Stanier's Black 5s (and from my experience of steam engines these are my favourite class to work on) but that site is now a supermarket. When I first moved to Perth, the building that housed the engineman's lodgings was still standing. However, there are improvements to the Highland main line ongoing so perhaps there will be an expansion of traffic too. Gleneagles Station may have lost some of its grandeur, but was renovated and the parking improved for the Ryder Cup tournament held at the nearby golf course.

It is 1986 and a Sunday afternoon walk to Perth station found a 26 and a 37 stabled at the north end of the station. In those days there were no barriers, and you could walk into and around the station at will. I do not recall what was in the numerous blue barrels present, perhaps anti-freeze. 26s were common locomotives in the area and for many years were, in pairs, the traction for Inverness to Edinburgh or Glasgow trains. By this time, 47s had taken over most of those duties.

An evening drive into the countryside allowed me to photograph this class 27 on oil tanks, no doubt bound for Grangemouth refinery. The 27 is accelerating away from the level crossing at Forteviot which is west of Hilton Junction on the line to Gleneagles and Stirling.

Speedlink was still in action and judging by the length and diversity of the load of this working, quite busy. The class 47 is working hard as it climbs out of Dunkeld. Going by the trees this is an early autumn view. The signal box can just be seen behind the freight and the semaphore signals are in use. As the loco is in rail blue this is, I think a mid-80s picture. There are now some useful footpaths in and around the area for taking photographs. The climb out of Dunkeld to the south is not to be taken lightly! Modellers take note of the different types of wagon that forms the train.

Perth station in the mid-1980s. This shows the way the station is configured to cater for the lines diverging east, across the River Tay for Dundee and Aberdeen whilst the main station has the lines for the north and Inverness, and at one time Aberdeen via Forfar. The class 27 has come in from Dundee and will be heading for Glasgow. The 37 may have come from Inverness or it might also be a Perth to Edinburgh working. Edinburgh could be reached either via Stirling or via Newburgh and Fife lines. A classic corporate blue era scene.

The arches at the south end of Perth station just ask for pictures like this to be taken. Such a view would be more difficult now as a lift and footbridge has been constructed to allow better access. In this view a class 27 is running out of the station, note that the driver is not passing a signal at danger as there is a subsidiary signal, the two white lights, allowing the red to be passed for shunting purposes.

The days of the class 27 were numbered when this picture was taken. This is a rail tour heading east bound for Inverness as I recall. The location is between Blackford and Gleneagles, parking the car was very difficult as the road is a very narrow one. I also caught the 27s again at Pitlochry later on that day.

In 1985 a Metro Cammell class 101 unit waits in the bay platforms to form an Edinburgh train. The station was undergoing a repaint and the end result was quite impressive. To the left of the picture can be seen the lines where locomotives and, as can be seen, coaches were stabled.

Dunkeld station is the location here. 47s had become the everyday power for Highland Line trains. Here is a large logo liveried example entering the station from the south, bound for Inverness. We can also see the semaphore signals controlling traffic at Dunkeld. The signal box and the semaphores are still in use at the time of writing. Turning right to head south on the A9 from Dunkeld Station, which is not in the town, is a tricky junction to negotiate.

A 47/7 in ScotRail livery on an Aberdeen to Glasgow train. The location is Errol Station which at the time this picture was taken had a small museum. The station is long closed to passengers and the goods sidings were also no longer in use. The museum is also no longer with us, and the station house is a private dwelling. There is a level crossing controlled by a signal box here which is still in use today. I note that the signals are off in both directions.

Errol station again but this time with a 47 in rail freight sector livery travelling light engine. The loco is 47 373 which would have been an Immingham engine at the time. It was an early casualty, suffering fire damage in 1991 and was scrapped at MC Metals in Glasgow a couple of years later. This shows the lights for the level crossing and a home signal at cab height. It is still possible to walk along the roadway in the picture. The footbridge in the picture is no longer accessible.

Hilton Junction signal box showing the lines for Newburgh to the left and Gleneagles to the right. A 47/7 is on a Glasgow to Aberdeen service and is about to enter Moncrieff Tunnel. Whilst this location would normally be off limits as it is Network Rail land, I had obtained permission to visit that day from British Transport Police. I liked the ScotRail livery applied to the 47/7s and matching stock.

A very typical Scottish scene, 27 002, with full snowploughs awaits its next turn in the bays at Perth Station. Again, this is mid-1980s and the 27s would not have much more time in traffic as by 1987 they would all be gone, apart from those few preserved. I am told that Scottish crews preferred 26s and 27s to the BR type 2s. I have driven classes 24, 25 and 26 at NYMR but not a 27.

The shape of things to come at Perth. A class 158 in 1993. These two car units replaced the loco hauled services to Aberdeen and Inverness. Having had to commute on these units I am not convinced that they were an improvement on what they replaced. The 158s have in their turn been ousted by class 170s although they remain in service with ScotRail. This particular unit will have undergone several livery changes in its days North of the Border.

This is the 2005 scene at Blackford which had boasted a station and yard, the remnants of which can be seen. As I write, the signal box and semaphores are still in use. This is an eastbound class 158 unit heading for Gleneagles and Perth and possibly further. The unit is in the 'Whoosh' (referring to the three coloured logo on the leading car) ScotRail livery. Happily, rail freight is returning to this location to take bottled water from the factory in the town

A GNER HST set bound for Inverness calls at Gleneagles. The station in its heyday was a most impressive structure and also boasted a yard, a line to Crieff and a branch to the hotel of the same name. Gleneagles Hotel was built as a railway hotel. Its presence meant that the station, now unstaffed, is still kept in good decorative order. The original entrance is a private house and the covered footbridges are long gone; however, the car park and approach road were upgraded and the station redecorated for the visit of the Ryder Cup golf competition to Gleneagles.

Gleneagles again but with a class 158 unit heading west. Not all trains stop at Gleneagles but this one had. As can be seen, the weather was a bit damp. The spacious station remains well kept. I travelled on 158s whilst commuting from Perth to Glasgow and wasn't overly impressed and bear in mind that these two car units replaced loco hauled sets of five or more carriages so overcrowding was common. The 158 is sporting a later livery which I think was the First Group's. Today all of ScotRail's units have the same livery which remains and only a small sticker denoting the operator of the day needs to be changed. Much simpler than redoing all the rolling stock.

We move north of Perth onto the Highland Line at Dunkeld. The signal box and semaphores remain in use at the time of writing. The station buildings are in commercial and not railway use and despite the A9 passing close by, the station has a very rural feel. This is a much more recent view and I had gone out to catch the last week of HST operation of the Kings Cross to Inverness service. The following week bi-mode units took over this working so another scene that is unlikely to be repeated. The Newcastle driver gave me a cheery wave as he passed through, I suspect that quite a few enthusiasts will have been out and about to capture the last week of HSTs on this duty.

Speedlink is still alive and kicking in this view as Eastfield's 37 403 pulls out of Crianlarich heading for Fort William. Crianlarich is the junction for the lines to Oban and Fort William. It also served the Callander & Oban line until that line's premature closure due to a rock fall in the 1960s. However, a stub of that line was still used for timber traffic at Crianlarich Lower, though that too has ceased. The sign points to the excellent tearooms on the station. 37 403 has carried the names *Isle of Mull*, *Glendarroch* and *Ben Cruachan*.

Kyle of Lochalsh station is busy with trains in both platforms. Class 37s are the regular engines having taken over from 26s. Just to the right of the photo was the docking area for the ferry across to Skye which could be a bottleneck in high season until the construction of the Skye bridge. The locomotive is 37 419 which was re-allocated from Inverness to Thornaby in 1991 so this view is between 1986 and 1991.

Another terminus, this time Oban, and again class 37s have taken over from BRCW type 2s. This was one of the pictures I didn't realise I had as it shows the train shed of Oban station still there. That has of course gone, and class 37s visit now and again on charters, the daily workings are all units. The skyline is dominated by McCaig's folly. Anyone who has studied law in Scotland will have had to read the case law relating to this structure during their course!

A classic West Highland scene, a corporate blue era 37 and coaches. This train has not long left Crianlarich and is heading for Oban on a glorious day. As can be imagined, this part of Scotland is very popular with hillwalkers and mountaineers as well as railway enthusiasts.

A blue class 37 heads west from Fort William bound for Mallaig. Another service now in the hands of class 156 units as we will see. The skyline is dominated by Ben Nevis and, as there is no snow on the top, this must be a summer's day. I have been to the top of 'the Ben' twice, a lengthy walk for sure but worth the effort for the view. Alas good weather and trips to Fort William do not always coincide as no doubt many fellow photographers will know.

It is 1985 and a friend and I braved the ferocious 'midgies' of Tyndrum to photograph the sleeper hauled by 37 043. Of interest is the converted class 25 to provide electric train heating for the sleepers and known as an 'ethel'. I think three class 25s were so converted. The service stopped at Tyndrum, hence the exhaust as it pulls away. Fast forward twenty years to image 175; same traction, no 'ethel', different stock but equally ravenous insects!

Now, I wonder just how much a rich tourist might pay for this trip up the West Highlands? In the days when this was taken, the likes of Real Time Trains wasn't on the go so workings such as this came as a surprise. 37 404 has an inspection saloon in tow and what views must be available to the occupants. I saw the working in the distance and was able to pull in to a lay-by to get the shot. O Gauge modellers will be able to recreate this working once the inspection saloon model becomes available, those modelling in OO already can.

Another surprise whilst driving to Fort William from Crianlarich was the appearance of this engineer's train. Again I was lucky enough to be able to stop the car and get a picture. The scenery here is vast and puts the railway into perspective. That said, you can still hear a class 37 coming! Corporate blue and the head-code box not plated over suggests a mid-80s scene

As the passenger train was timetabled, we were able to choose a location rather than be surprised. We are west of Tyndrum and have walked some way along from the road to get the train properly in the magnificent landscape. We heard the 37 coming before we saw it. A 37 on Mk1s, a typical formation for a Fort William to Glasgow Queen Street service. Nowadays this would be a 156 possibly with the newly introduced single unit bicycle carriers.

Just to show that it was not all class 37s at Fort William, we found a class 20 working and I think it had been out to Corpach but was now back shunting in and around Fort William as the 'off' ground signal shows. It was quite unusual to see a lone class 20, at least in the Central Belt. Shunting with one cannot have been easy as the forward vision along the bonnet is not the best.

The sign here says it all, Crianlarich again, the line for Oban and Crianlarich Lower diverges to the left whilst the 37 on a speedlink service is on the line for Tyndrum Upper and Fort William. Freight in the form of GBRF class 66 and its train of Alumina tanks from North Blyth still runs to Fort William, 6S45 loaded and 6E45 empties. Indeed, this flow passes my house overlooking the Edinburgh Sub!

The inevitable class 37 hard at work on what I am sure was a charter given the livery of the coaches, climbs to County March summit having traversed Horseshoe Curve. The scenery in this part of the world is so spectacular, alas the weather is not always so pleasant. The loco is 37 402 which was named *Oor Wullie* in December 1985.

Another 37, this time 37 410, on a freight which includes fuel oil. This shows the goods that used to be moved by rail and there was a fuel depot at Fort William to accept train loads of fuel. That traffic has been lost to rail, but one wonders if it will return given the need to reduce carbon emissions. This working has breasted the summit and is on its way to Tyndrum Upper. I did photograph freights when they appeared on these lines; just as well, given that they seem to be a thing of the past here (except for the alumina flow). Modellers might be interested to see what the consist of these mixed flow trains was and the types of wagons used.

Class 37, 37 423, in a freight sector livery, is heading for Mallaig on the West Highland extension. I was blessed with decent weather on this occasion and between trains was able to have a quick paddle in the sea at the amazing Morar beach. The road for Mallaig has been considerably improved since my first trips. Of course, this route too is now the preserve of class 156 units but does see locomotives regularly on 'The Jacobite' and other charters.

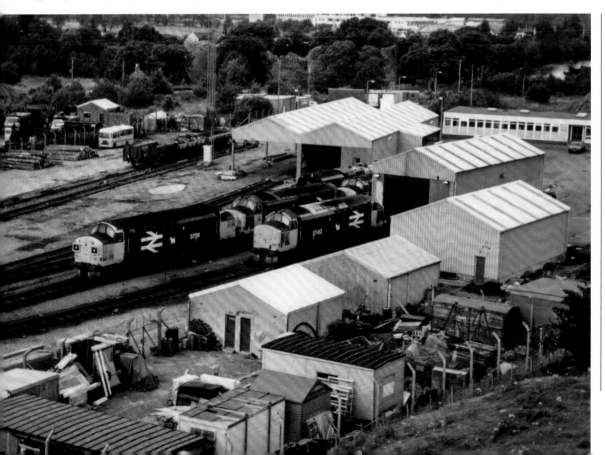

This is an unusual view of the shed at Fort William and class 37s are the mainstay of traction with 37 412 and 37 011 in the company of two other class mates. Also on shed is a Stanier Black 5 for the steam hauled service to Mallaig but I don't think it had acquired the 'Jacobite' name when this photograph was taken. The bus in the background looks quite an interesting vehicle. The West Highland extension can be seen curving away at the left hand corner of the view.

The terminus of the extension at Mallaig. The road from Fort William to Mallaig has seen considerable improvement since the date of this trip which I think was in the early 1980s, one of the improvements being the approach to the town which uses what was railway ground but on this visit the old layout was still in place and what remained of the engine shed still stood and was worth recording. I don't think this building lasted much longer.

I managed one or two day trips up to Fort William and Mallaig and on this occasion we find a class 37 at Mallaig waiting to return to Fort William. Steam heating is still the order of the day and the hose suggests that some topping up with water was going on. These trains would in time be turned over to class 156 units which are still in use today but I do wonder if a loco hauled set would provide more seats, better views and more room for bicycles and thus a better service. As well as The Jacobite, the West Highlands remain a popular destination for charter trains.

We move to another Highland terminus that at Kyle of Lochalsh. I did not experience the days of class 26s and 27s on these routes, however they were still loco hauled with class 37s in charge and it looks like this is one of Inverness's own 37 415. In the background is the drill tower of Highlands and Islands Fire Brigade's Kyle of Lochalsh fire station. The train looks like it is heading into the Up platform.

Another view at Kyle of Lochalsh this time looking down onto the station's Down platform. Again the traction is an Inverness 37/4, the stag emblem of the depot being just visible on the back cabside. The coaching stock is worth looking at here as it is in a distinct livery used for a while on the line of green and white (which was also used on the West Highland line) rather than blue and white and we can see that an attempt at an observation car of sorts has been made by adding a Metro Cammell DMU car to the set. I do wonder if observation cars might make a return for highly scenic lines.

Use of a 'Highland Travel Pass' allowed you on trains, buses and ferries all across the region. As a result, I was able to visit both termini on the Far North line. Again I missed loco hauled services so it was a 156 unit that took us to Thurso. This has been my one and only visit here having made it only as far as Inverness since. This trip also allowed me to hop on the ferry to visit Orkney, coming straight back on the same ferry.

The same week but a much brighter day took us to Wick. Again the trip was by 156 and I see from the picture that this unit was rather coy about displaying its number. As I recall we caught the same train back to Inverness. Trips like this really do underline just how far from the central belt Inverness is and then just how much further on Wick and Thurso are!

Another image from the same tour around the Highlands and Islands. I am so glad that I decided to use the ticket to cross from Oban to Mull and visit the narrow gauge railway there. There was steam and diesel traction on offer and as I recall a fair number of passengers wanting a run. Alas this venture is no longer operating, so another scene unlikely to be repeated. I don't now recall if I had time to take a trip on the Isle of Mull railway as, again, I was taking the ferry straight back to Oban that day.

A later view of Mallaig. The approach road has been completed and new buildings have sprung up where the engine shed and turntable had been. The turntable is sadly missed; just how useful might that be today for steam locos and observation cars? The 156 unit leading has a snow plough fitted but this was a fine day (once I had reached Fort William) and the sunshine enhanced the real majesty of the scenery in this part of Scotland. The good weather allowed another visit to the white sands of Morar beach!

The date stamp on the print tells me this view is from July or August 2005. The class 37s' lengthy run on the sleeper to Fort William was coming to an end. Contrast this view with picture 157 where the 37 also had a converted 25 'Ethel' in tow. By this time the 37s were equipped with ETH. I managed to take a day's leave and was up very early to drive up to Tyndrum to record a 37 on the sleepers for the last time before 67s took over. Now this sort of photography is not for the faint of heart and I was mightily relieved that the train was bang on time as my appearance brought forth a veritable swarm of 'midgies' making the short wait for the 37 to appear a most uncomfortable experience.

I had ventured to Fort William to see "The Jacobite", an early start so once fortified with breakfast from the cafe at Fort William station I recorded the sleeper stock which had been shunted out of the platforms and the loco run round ready to be shunted back into a platform later in the day. The sleeper still runs but with rather different traction. 37s still appear in Fort William but in connection with charter trains. Unusually for photographic trips, all had gone to plan that day!

CHAPTER 9
CENTRAL SCOTLAND

I think my first trip into Central Scotland was to a rail show at Stirling. The SRPS J36 *Maude* was there and *Union of South Africa* was supposed to be there but was running very late. I did see it but only through the front window of the DMU we were travelling home on! Mentioning the SRPS, in those days they were still based at Wallace Street Goods Yard in Falkirk which I visited a couple of times.

Subsequently, I did make a couple of trips to Stirling as it was still relatively busy, had semaphore signals and loco hauled services passing through. Like everywhere else units took over and I was through Stirling many times whilst commuting to Glasgow. I did make one visit to catch the ScotRail 'whoosh' livery before it was changed as a new operator took over. Much later, I went there to have a trip on the reopened Alloa line. Much has changed with fewer platforms in use and no more semaphore signals and of course almost no locomotives to be seen save for the occasional freight workings.

Another location which was well worth a visit was Grangemouth shed, still a busy depot with freight work from the nearby refinery and docks. Rail blue dominated and a weekend visit would find a mix of 08s 20s, 27s and 37s. The shed was the old steam shed. Whilst the docks and refinery are still there the shed is not; however, it remains a site of railway interest as DRS run freightliners for a logistics firm from there and other operators have intermodal services to and from the port. I never encountered any problems getting round Grangemouth.

One of the places I visited for work was Forfar where I had lived as a boy between 1960 and 1970. One day I took my camera to record what had been the railway yards and station. The station building was still there in part as was the engine shed but the rest of the area was a wilderness. Today the site is mainly a housing estate with some industrial units including Forfar shed which is still in use and one of the very few steam sheds still standing North of the Border.

A very typical scene of its time, a class 101 (although we never referred to DMUs by their class but by their manufacturer or place of manufacture) Metro Cammell DMU makes a characteristic smoke screen departure from Stirling. These units were the most common to be seen in the east, however there was a significant allocation of Derby units in the west. Cravens and Gloucester units were less numerous. The infrastructure of the steam era is still in place as regards semaphore signalling.

Class 47s were common enough at Stirling working to Aberdeen and Inverness, however the livery of this example caught my eye as it is certainly very different to the norm and may well have been unique to this loco. That said, class 47s have seen very many liveries over the years. The loco is 47 522 which was named *Doncaster Enterprise* in 1987. It had a rather chequered history as it suffered serious damage after colliding with a tractor at Forteviot in May of 1982, was rebuilt only to be involved in another collision at Dover at the end of 1989

A class 37 in large logo livery leaves Stirling for the south, another common sight of the times was the gas holder. The sidings to the right of the picture look little used but as late as the early 1980s these roads would hold a fair number of vanfits. Whilst vegetation is evident in the little used sidings, the main line is still clear of greenery, a contrast to some lines today.

This view is taken from Stirling station and we see an approaching HST, the power car's livery not matching the coaching stock. This will be an Inverness working. The complexity of the signalling is evident too. The post that the HST is about to pass has home and distant arms and also a smaller shunting signal. Spotting semaphores at night must have been a very difficult task especially if confronted with a large gantry. Stirling is of course now colour lights.

A 2001 visit to Stirling brings a view of a Derby unit with a head-code. Many similar units were built without the head-code box which if memory serves me correctly were for suburban services rather than longer distance trips. I am not sure why the cab window surrounds were highlighted in black, it looked in keeping with the Strathclyde PTE livery but not with the corporate blue and white. The signalling again is of interest showing the main and subsidiary signals, perhaps a useful reference for modellers.

Another class 47 heading north but this is in a much more common large logo livery; this service would be for Aberdeen or Inverness. The loco is 47 633, once more had it appeared in Stirling in the 1970s it would not have been common at all as it started out as D1668 then 47 083 *Orion*, one of the Western Region allocated named Brush 4s. On this occasion, the driver will have noted that whilst the home signal arm is at proceed, the distant arm is at caution so the next along signal will be at danger. This also is from the 2001 visit to Stirling.

The last image from my 2001 visit shows another class 47 this time heading south and in yet another livery this time the 'Inter City' version. The loco's number is in small black numerals at the bottom of the cabside, not the easiest to see. It is 47 804. The rails suggest that the bay platforms had not been used recently.

We move to Grangemouth MPD. The shed was still the old steam era building and at the weekend would contain a fair number of engines. This view inside the shed shows a class 20 and a class 37, frequent residents of the shed. The 20 is of the later version with a head-code box as opposed to the discs fitted to earlier examples. On a weekday the shed would be all but empty.

I thought it unusual to see a clean 'Inter City' liveried class 47 at Grangemouth on the same day as the 20 was captured on film inside the shed. This engine has an ex works look to it. The shed would also have 08s, type 2s and 37s stabled. There was considerable traffic in the area, not least that from the refinery. Today the shed has gone but the site is still a rail location for liners operated mainly by DRS. Oil traffic is now in the hands of Colas.

A general view of the front of the shed gives us a typical selection of motive power with a class 26, 26 041 bearing the West Highland Terrier of Eastfield shed, a class 20 with the earlier disc head-codes and two class 37s. The 26 has seen some refurbishment as the original front has had the connecting doors plated over and the head-code discs removed. Sector liveries have also started to appear as on the full head-code 37. Grangemouth wasn't the only shed to still use the steam age buildings; when I visited Polmadie, Dundee and Motherwell sheds they were still steam age buildings. Modellers may be interested in the smoke staining of the shed front and the relative tidiness of the yards.

A classic Scottish loco on shed at Grangemouth, Eastfield's 27 026 rests in what looks like evening sunlight, a class that would be a common sight at this shed. It sports corporate rail blue livery whilst the 37 in the background is in large logo blue. Whilst some of the class 26 fleet made it into sector liveries the 27s did not.

I was sent to work in the Forfar office for a week in the late 1980s and having seen that the station and shed were still standing in a derelict area I took my camera to record the buildings. The shed appears to be in use of some sort and part of the roof has been refurbished but I thought it would be a good idea to record the scene in case it was pulled down. As fortune would have it the shed was not demolished and as will be seen in the next image it is still standing and in use.

I decided on a nostalgia trip up to Forfar one day. Whilst the rail over bridge on the way to Station Park has gone and the station buildings have been replaced by housing and much of the land that was railway yard is also built on for industrial use, there is no mistaking the presence of the typical Caledonian style engine shed still standing at Forfar and still in use as a steel fabricator's. Another location that might make a fine subject for a model and it would be possible to take accurate measurements of the shed.

I had decided to visit Stirling station but I am not sure if this was due to the possibility of the semaphore signals going or the ScotRail livery on the units changing. Either way, we see a class 156 entering from the north end. The date is October 2004, so the Alloa branch had not been reinstated by then. The fine semaphore signals are to the fore and the station signs have the ScotRail 'whoosh' branding too.

A class 170 unit is about to head south from the main platforms at Stirling. This was quite an impressive station with bay and through platforms and of course, in BR steam days Stirling had its own shed with an allocation of some forty or so locos but by the mid-60s that was down to single figures. That was the old Caledonian shed, the NBR also had a shed in Stirling called Shore Road. Interesting to muse that, if this 170 was a service for Glasgow, in the 1960s it may well have been A4 hauled! Stirling of course also saw Stanier pacifics en route to and from Perth.

Another success at reopening railways is shown here with a class 158 at Alloa. Reinstating this line allows a circular route through Fife, across the Forth Bridge and via Dalmeny and Winchburgh Junctions back to Central Scotland which is a popular route for steam charters which can also then access the SRPS at Boness. Longannet Power Station could also be found on the route and, whilst it is long closed, the site is earmarked for a new train building factory. There was regular coal traffic to the power station, especially after the closure of the colliery of the same name.

The same day we see a view of Stirling station including a 158 unit. The semaphore signals remain in use. That is no longer the case as colour lights now control Stirling. This view of the south end of the station shows just how extensive the layout, is boasting ten platforms. For a short while there was some experimentation with starting a London train from Stirling. Of course in earlier times, Stirling would also have had traffic using the Callander and Oban lines.

CHAPTER 10
WEST COAST MAIN LINE & CARLISLE

It was not unheard of for the Scottish Railfans Society to do an overnight observation of the WCML at Lamington so busy was the line at night, principally with freight. One of the men who appeared in Waverley from time to time of a Saturday also did overnight 'obbo' at Carstairs. I personally never partook. Carstairs was a busy junction as trains could head west to Motherwell and Glasgow, Mossend and Central Scotland, north to Stirling or east to Edinburgh. The first memory I have of travelling in that direction was that ballast changed from a grey colour locally to red on the WCML. Carstairs was still a stabling point and the Edinburgh bound passenger services changed from electric to diesel traction. The train would come in to the station from the south electric hauled, the diesel came onto what was the rear of the train, the electric loco came off, a tail lamp was put on what was now the rear of the train and the service was right away for the capital and almost straight into the bank to the top of Cobbinshaw. This is a bank not to be trifled with; it is a steep climb from Carstairs up to the reservoir and worse in the other direction as the climb isn't as steep but is much longer so double headed 37s on freightliners would be at walking pace by the summit.

It was also common for trains to have Edinburgh and Glasgow portions which either split or conjoined at Carstairs. The splitting wasn't too bad but some of the coupling of the two sets of coaches was robust. Now I know from working with A4 pacific *Sir Nigel Gresley* at NYMR and support crewing with West Coast that getting the buckeye couplings to grip does require a certain amount of force. However, at Carstairs you would certainly not want to have a cup of tea in hand whilst the shunting was afoot! The Edinburgh portions were mainly 47 hauled but other classes, such as 37s, sometimes appeared. All this changed when the route for Edinburgh, including the very tight curve of the station avoiding line was electrified. The practice of having portions reduced too, though of course the sleepers still carry out this move at Carstairs. This meant that services could stay electric hauled (involving a run round if the service was due to call at Carstairs) throughout and electric locos began to visit Edinburgh from the west, as I recall usually 86s and then later on 90s. Freight remained diesel hauled for Edinburgh in the main as the Sub wasn't (and still isn't) electrified.

I very rarely was in Glasgow in my early days and can only vaguely recall the Class 50s double heading the principal WCML services. Polmadie depot was still the steam shed structure and I did visit a couple of times. Our Scottish Railfans tours often involved the use of overnight trains out of Glasgow Central. I also visited Motherwell shed (still the steam shed building) a couple of times. We did attend a St Rollox works open day where there were a lot of stored Class 17s and where, for 50p, a Forfar totem was purchased.

On down the WCML proper and the first point of interest were the loops at Abington which might hold a freight. These loops are still very much in use today. On the first couple of trips to down the WCML there were still bankers at Beattock in the form of a couple of class 20s. But that didn't last long and very soon traffic had to attempt Beattock on its own.

There remain loops at the summit. Approaching Carlisle, New Yard was still busy and had a stabling point and then Kingmoor shed. Like Millerhill, New yard is but a shadow of what it was in the 1970s, but Kingmoor is still a depot for DRS. As I recall, the power station just past Kingmoor had an industrial shunter before entering Citadel. On my first visits, the freight avoiding lines were still functioning so we headed for Dentonholme North Junction where we could watch what was coming and going from the north end of the station and the freights. Carlisle was included in the Freedom of Scotland rover ticket and for a time Kingmoor and Canal sheds had Scottish shed codes, 68A and 68E.

Kingmoor and then New Yard were a fair trek from the city centre. On one occasion I had actually obtained a permit for Kingmoor, half way down the drive to the shed a window was thrown open and, I assume the foreman, shouted several times 'you can't come round here'. He was quite surprised when we got up to the window and I produced the permit! That was my one and only visit to Kingmoor.

The alternative route to Carlisle from Scotland via Dumfries is one which I have travelled on but have only visited a couple of times to watch diversions or a steam charter. It is also one of the parts of the country that I do not have photographs of. Carlisle remains a busy place now and still attracts enthusiasts. I am quite often in Carlisle with West Coast and have headed north on the footplate of *Scots Guardsman* a couple of times. As with most stations, loco hauled passenger trains are few and far between, most services being units. However, there is the attraction of the freight which now runs through Citadel as the avoiding lines were closed some years back after a serious derailment.

One of the regular freight workings on the West Coast was the fuel tank workings between Grangemouth and Dalston. It was a booked Class 60 working and did sometimes run on a Saturday. I quite often took a run down to the line near to Crawford to watch the railway activity. In those days you could readily access the banking above the viaduct at Crawford. This is the viewpoint for 60 023 on 6S36 the empty bogie tanks from Dalston, which is on the Cumbrian Coast line, to Grangemouth, a long and heavy train so ideal for a class 60. This is another picture which you could not take today. The flow is no longer operated by EWS or DB, class 60s are not the booked traction and fencing has been erected which prevents access to the location.

Another typical sight of the time is a Virgin Trains class 90 and matching set which will include at the other end of the train a DVT so that loco run rounds were not required. This train is heading north having just crossed the River Clyde and that particular bridge featured in some of Derek Cross's photographic work.

Virgin Trains also operated HST sets on the WCML and this is a sight that you cannot repeat today. The location is just off the A702 just north of Lamington Viaduct over the River Clyde. That bridge caused significant delays a few years back when severe flooding damaged its structure. It was only by good fortune that there wasn't a serious incident. The HST is heading south.

A class 87 but this time in blue livery and intercity stock so pre Virgin Trains days. The 87s were the front line locos for the Euston to Glasgow Express trains. The location is between Crawford and Abington. A back road runs alongside the line, so it is easy enough to get to. However, the ever present fencing has since been erected and many of the locations that I used to use in this area are no longer accessible.

Another picture at Crawford and some refurbishment of the viaduct structure is ongoing and a temporary yard has been created for that work. The freightliner, most likely for Coatbridge is in the hands of a single class 90 in the two tone grey livery. The class 90s have carried quite a few liveries over the years. Very often these liners were double headed with either class 86s or 90s. The 86s are no longer plying their trade but 90s are. With freightliners being operated by DRS, DB and GBRF, class 66, 68 and 88 locos can also be seen on such trains.

Now, I know that this location is not on the WCML, however I wanted to include an image of the very sorry state into which the Station Hotel at Ayr has fallen. It has lain empty for many years and is now in a state of considerable disrepair to the extent that it has caused closures at Ayr station due to falling masonry. As can be seen, some work has been undertaken to prevent this. A unit waits for departure in the through platforms. The state of the building is a huge pity as it is a most impressive piece of railway architecture.

A Virgin Trains West Coast Main Line service formed of a class 87, coaches and DVT tackles Beattock. Certainly no need for a banker, not that one would be available and the passengers will barely notice they are climbing. It is even more the case today on Pendolino units. This picture does convey just how relatively remote the line is as there is nothing much in the way of habitation nearby.

A similar train but travelling through the town of Beattock. There is no station, no shed only the remnants of the branch to Moffat and no bankers waiting their next duty. The lines other than the main line do not look like they have seen use for some time. On my first few trips down this stretch of line there were still bankers in the form of class 20 diesels but even that remnant of the steam era importance of this site has gone.

Just south of Abington we find a pair of Class 90s on a parcels working. EWS were hoping to expand the Royal Mail services by rail, however that did not happen. Mail still travels by rail but in specially adapted EMU sets. Perhaps mail and parcels in particular will return to rail but not in a format like this. The morning was quite misty as I recall and the line quite busy with both freight and passenger workings.

Not long after the 90s had passed on their postal, the distinctive sound of a 37 could be heard approaching from the south. It turned out to be a pair of 37s operated by Direct Rail Services, a company set up pretty much in house by British Nuclear Fuels on privatisation of the railways for the transport of nuclear flasks. These flasks will have come from Sellafield on the Cumbrian Coast line and would be destined for either Hunterston 'B' or Torness Power Stations. Flask trains still run but with class 68s and only to Torness as Hunterston 'B' has very recently been shut down.

We are slightly further north towards the loops at Abington and find a pair of class 92 locos on a mixed freight including car transporters and china clay wagons for the paper industry. This consist will most likely have gone to Mossend Yard where the various portions would be split for onward transmission. The locomotives themselves were very powerful and for electrics quite noisy at times. One of their more recent uses has been on the Caledonian Sleepers but as a class they seem to have been underused, not fulfilling their original promise.

This is Abington where there are loops on both lines. On a couple of occasions I have been on a support crew taking water in the down loop. Here a Class 60 on an engineer's train has been looped to allow faster passenger services to pass. The Class 60 is limited to 60mph so loops will be familiar to the locos and their drivers. Once again the sector decal has been replaced by an EWS three beasties one. As I recall, this particular train had to wait some while for at least three passenger trains to pass. It is bound for Carlisle.

It is 1985 and as far as I am aware this is the first railway picture taken after acquiring my Fujica SLR camera, a real upgrade as it has in built light metering. The subject matter is a class 25 on freight and this was an everyday sight in those days. Rail blue was the livery of the day and I think it suited most locomotives. The same view today would show refurbishment of the station roofing and canopies but otherwise would be similar. This is the platform into which our steam charters often arrive, so I suspect that many of today's photographers will have pictures of *Galatea*, *Scots Guardsman* and the like in the same position as the 25.

The same visit shows blue electrics. The wires hadn't come anywhere near Edinburgh at this point so for electrics you had to get across to a point on the WCML. Here are a pair of class 86s on freight. It is interesting to note that pairs of 86s have only recently been ousted from freightliner work by pairs of class 90s. Some of the smaller classes of AC electrics were still on the go too. A visit to Carlisle in those days certainly filled up the notebook!

Just to show it wasn't all 86s and 87s, 85 005 (and this is the only picture of a class 85 that I have) put in an appearance on what looks like either a parcels or a newspaper train. For an electric loco these particular engines made quite a bit of noise. There seemed to be so much more variety of traction around and still plenty of loco hauled trains. I do wish that I had recorded more images, however slide film and processing wasn't cheap so you really had to think about what you were taking; a far cry from the digital age we have now!

These roads to the west side of Citadel used to provide a stabling point for locos between turns. On this occasion a Derby built DMU waits in the platform in this 1990 view. Stabled but still running is 31 342 I do not recall seeing this class in Carlisle at all frequently which most likely drew my attention. Also in view is 60 006 and these were common visitors to Carlisle, this one in original livery. The last class 60 I saw in Carlisle was in Colas livery working the log train for Chirk, but that duty is now a class 70 turn.

A view of contrasts here for sure, or perhaps the tortoise and the hare. An 08 shunter on an engineer's working sits beside a Pendolino running south not stopping at Carlisle. Again this is a picture which cannot be repeated today. Whilst the Pendolino will still be in traffic it will no longer be in Virgin Trains livery and will be due for a refit under the new operator Avanti West Coast and the number of class 08s in service has dwindled further and seeing them out and about like this is most unusual.

Carlisle Citadel remains a busy station although changing locos as used to happen on a regular basis in steam days doesn't happen today. However, it is still a crew change point for several companies. Working on West Coast support crews I have become quite familiar with the station and the surrounding lines. This image is from 2003 and who could resist a picture of a Royal train liveried Class 47 on Pullman stock? This special working (and many of these pass through Carlisle) provided some variety of traction and rolling stock. Class 47s can still be found on charter trains but not perhaps as well turned out as this one.

On the same visit as the previous picture I found one of the Royal Mail EMU sets. It will have come from Shieldmuir at Motherwell. These units are still in service. The class 56 that can be seen in the sidings however probably not so, although there are still a handful of these machines at work. It used to be quite common for several locos to be stabled there; nowadays usually the only occupant is a DRS 57 which acts as a 'Thunderbird'.

At the north end of Citadel we see north and southbound expresses, both Virgin Trains sets but one has a class 90 powering from the rear of its train and the class 87 heading its train. Nowadays Pendolinos and Voyagers provide the stock for the WCML passenger services. As I do not recall steam on BR, my earliest recollection of WCML trains are of class 50s in rail blue, usually double heading.

Further evidence that parcels traffic or RES (rail express systems) was still going by rail and a class 67 is in charge, very much ideal work for this class with a high turn of speed. The stock it is hauling will now, I suspect, be long gone. I discovered in reviewing my photographs that I do not have many pictures of this class at work. Class 67s were used as 'thunderbird' locos at strategic locations up and down the ECML but again that is a duty that no longer exists.

Something I did not expect to find in the bay platform at the north end of Carlisle was a class 31. The bay platforms at the north end of the station usually holds units bound for Scotland via the Dumfries route. I think I am right that this is in 'Fragonset' livery but there were quite a few changes in quick succession as to which firm operated these locos. I suppose that they were always unusual sights to me since they appeared only very rarely back home and whilst they were seen in the Newcastle area, I don't recall seeing them as often at Carlisle.

Since the freight avoiding lines were closed following a fairly nasty derailment, all the freight for Kingmoor and New Yard goes through the station. Here we have another pair of class 92s, the consist again has the slurry tankers with raw materials for the paper making industry. Trains of this material still run today and Aberdeen is one of the destinations. The class 92s are dual voltage and can pick up from third rail or overhead equipment, features necessary for their intended use on Channel tunnel workings.

This is another 2003 picture, we can see a class 90 and some parcels stock the coach in the picture is one of those fitted out with driving controls. The main interest however is a blue class 37 on a coal train. The 37 had been repainted specially into BR blue livery. Of course, coal trains of this type are no more.

This unusual pairing caught my interest as we have a 56 leading a 66 (which I think must have failed as it was silent as the train passed). The 56 of course was far from silent as it accelerated away! I am not sure what the load of this particular working was.

Direct Rail Services acquired and then modified several class 20s for their flask trains. This pair, whilst carrying new numbers, do not appear to have received the modifications. Once again, seeing DRS class 20s will soon be a thing of the past as DRS recently announced their intention to dispose of their class 20 fleet. Also consigned to history is the travelling post office stock in the background.

It is 2004 and we have a pair of class 37s on a charter train at the north end of the station; the locos are hauling a 'Pathfinder' tour and are in their classic EWS livery. The picture also shows the very fine buildings at that end of Citadel and the front of a class 156 unit waiting to work a service over the old Glasgow & South Western route to Scotland. Note also the 156 is sporting the Strathclyde PTE livery rather than the ScotRail brand.

Above left: This is the same Pathfinder rail tour which is about to honour long gone traditions of a Carlisle engine change. I have been told by my NYMR colleagues Bob Bullock and Pete Hanson that these engine changes kept the Polmadie engines, particularly their Scots, North of the Border and meant that in their native Northamptonshire they stood no chance of seeing, for example 46102 *Black Watch*. Bob, by then a Kettering engineman did see it, withdrawn, on a visit to Corkerhill but it eluded Pete. There is a class 67 waiting to take over and this study in front ends presented itself and was too tempting a photograph not to take.

Above right: I have noted earlier that unusual combinations of locos would almost always be worth a photo. Again, this is a 2004 image and I certainly found it most unusual to see a class 92 coupled to an EWS liveried class 47. However, a freightliner coal train (note the advent of newer higher capacity wagons) passed at just the wrong time, or so I thought. The coal train must have been due a crew change as it stopped and two wagon ends framed this most unlikely pairing.

Below: That same day, a bread and butter MGR coal train appeared, hauled by the ubiquitous 66. Now I confess that I am not a particular fan of class 66s so have tended not to photograph them, however it was becoming clear that the days of this type of wagon was numbered so an opportunity to record them had to be taken when it arose. This also shows that there are bi directional lines at Carlisle. Indeed, the railways around Carlisle are varied and complex as I have discovered working with West Coast support crews during our various moves shunting stock and going to and from Upperby to service and water our engine.

CHAPTER 11
PRESERVATION

My first recollection of preservation in the early to mid-1970s was of visiting the SRPS then at Wallace Street yard in Falkirk. After considering other potential sites, the SRPS moved to their current home at Bo'ness and began to construct the facilities they now enjoy. The emerging Strathspey Railway was also running but visiting came in much later years, mainly due to the distance between Aviemore and Edinburgh.

I recall doing one Sunday's work volunteering at Wallace Street but getting there and back by train on a Sunday wasn't particularly easy and was time consuming. Closer to home was Prestongrange in East Lothian so once I was able to drive, Sunday afternoons were spent there, digging the ground, laying and maintaining track and operating our unique steam loco, a Grant Ritchie 0-4-2 tank. When it was retired at the end of its boiler certificate we used an Andrew Barclay 0-4-0 tank, No 6 which is currently on loan to the SRPS. I still have connections with Prestongrange but most of my preserved railway activity has been at Grosmont.

As the years went by, other Heritage sites grew up, most reflecting the industrial past however ex BR projects such as the Caledonian Railway at Brechin also appeared. Many museums across the country hold items of railway interest as befits a country with a considerable history of locomotive building. Today there is a fine choice of sites including industrial, ex BR, museums static exhibits and narrow gauge lines. I confess that there are places I have still to visit or have not visited in many years, Alford and Leadhills being examples.

The locomotives, both steam and diesel, at Aviemore, Bo'ness and Brechin reflect (in the main) the traction that was in use in Scotland. Aviemore also has a genuine BR shed to operate from. Main line connections allow main line registered locos to visit particularly at Bo'ness. From my perspective, I really do not recall steam on BR, so it is great to see and hear say a class 26 working again. Happily, I have had the opportunity to drive a 26 at The Moors and the questionable privilege of coupling two diesels both fitted with full snowploughs!

The Strathspey Railway at Aviemore is blessed with the use of the original shed from steam days. They are another railway with plans to extend which are coming to fruition. However, this was the scene in 2001. The line's Black 5 looks a bit forlorn but fast forward twenty years and it is back in steam after a lengthy and detailed restoration. It is also an ideal loco for the line and of course Black 5s were numerous on the Highland Main Line. It is also important to retain, if possible, original structures such as the shed.

Another, but earlier, visit to the Strathspey was made, this time in winter to see a more unusual resident in the shape of a class 44, one of the original 'Peaks' D8 or 44 008 and there was a plan to rename it *Schiehallion* after a Scottish mountain. That name was used on a Class 60 some years later. However, the 44 has since returned south. These are real heavy weight machines so perhaps not really suited to the Strathspey line. Also in view is an Ivatt 2-6-0, 46464 which has now moved to Brechin but the Strathspey now operate 46512 from the same class. The Peak dwarfs the Ruston 48 also in the picture.

The next visit I paid to Aviemore was by train and it is still a long trip from Edinburgh. Pictured in the Strathspey Railway part of Aviemore Station is Caledonian 0-6-0 BR number 57566 in BR black. It is the only example of its class remaining. We will see this locomotive again but in Caledonian Blue later on at Bo'ness. This engine has been a regular performer over the years and it does seem to me suitable that a Caledonian Railway locomotive should be working at this railway. The Strathspey benefits from a connection with Network rail lines.

Also in steam that day was the Ivatt 2-6-0 46512 and it is captured here running round the stock to form the next service train. This is an ideal loco for the type of work required on the line. Being a more modern design it provides rather better protection from the elements for the crew than the Caley 0-6-0. You do have to wonder about conditions for enginemen in the days of little more than a cab front as protection from a winter's night on the Highland Main line. I am sure that is something today's steam crews would rather not re-create!

One of the more recent, relatively, preserved lines is that of the Caledonian Railway (Brechin) Ltd. This picture is the northern end of the railway at Bridge of Dun. As well as the line onwards to Montrose and Aberdeen there was also a line from here to Guthrie, Forfar and Perth. The class 08, D3059 and named *Brechin City*, a reference to the town's football club, is a very useful machine for not only shunting but engineer's and permanent way trains. The rolling stock also looks the part, especially given the former status of this station.

This was the scene at Brechin, which does have a cathedral, hence the football team's name, and we can see a wagon body in front of the shed, which also shows the extent of the site, a class 27, a type which would often have visited the line and the then resident Ivatt 2-6-0 46464 known as 'The Carmylie Pilot' a loco with a long association with the area. The railway has progressed well since this picture was taken. On this visit nothing was running as I recall.

The railway's diesel galas draw visitors to the line who might not otherwise make the trip. On this occasion a class 37 and 26 are double heading and arriving into the terminus at Brechin. The fine station exterior is to be complemented with reinstatement of platform coverings. As I recall it was a good day out and an experience that I will repeat. It is always interesting to see what progress railways have made between visits, especially when those visits are years apart.

Grant Ritchie 0-4-2 tank at work on a running day at Prestongrange. The extra axle allows for a much more spacious cab and easier coal storage for work. This was our engine for use on running days. It is a unique example. The engine had worked at Lady Victoria Pit before being moved to what was a mining museum with the beam engine as its central exhibit. The site changed focus somewhat when Lady Victoria was opened as a mining museum so Prestongrange now reflects the wider industrial heritage of the area. Sadly, the Grant Ritchie has been out of use for many years and I doubt that it will work again. That is a great shame as it is a very elegant locomotive.

A busy scene at Prestongrange. The track was laid and maintained by hand. The track layout belies the mass of bricks and other materials that used to cover the site, all moved pretty much by hand. This view shows one of the NCB internal user wagons sandwiched by No 6 an Andrew Barclay 0-4-0 and a simplex motor rail diesel which is privately owned. No 6 was used as our engine after No 7's, the Grant Ritchie, boiler certificate expired. No 6 has been on long term loan at Bo'ness and its boiler certificate has now also expired

As the site of a former colliery and brickworks, there will have been narrow gauge lines on the go and this short length of track was installed to allow us to run this Hudson Hunslet 2ft gauge loco. A couple of friends had bought it from a scrap yard and it was restored in my parent's garage before being moved to Prestongrange. From there it was sold privately but is now back in action this time at Lathalmond.

This is a steam 'navvie', a Marshall Fleming built mobile steam crane. As well as doing all the things a crane can do, this machine is also self propelling by steam. The out riggers were for dock working. When I started at Prestongrange, the Marshall Fleming was still in working order and was steamed on a fairly regular basis. It was a bit tricky to 'drive' as you were never quite sure which way the engine would go. Like many of the exhibits at Prestongrange, it is most unlikely to be returned to steam.

This is the line running alongside the coast road at Prestongrange, built by hand, which allows access from the old pit baths which serves as an engine shed to the main running line. The locomotive, a Ruston 88, has just arrived from its former home with ICI at Dumfries. Clearly the staff at ICI had decided to name their loco *Ivor*, but this locomotive's whistle would not allow the engine into any male voice choir! An interesting machine which has a donkey engine that drives a compressor charging a cylinder and the main engine is turned over with that compressed air. Quite a procedure for starting it up. The Prestongrange site is earmarked for some development with a purpose built shed for the railway exhibits included in the plans.

Visiting engines are all part and parcel of preserved lines, Bo'ness being no different. On this trip to the railway, the visitor was the diminutive *Joem*. A fine station pilot but I am not sure that it would be suitable for a full round trip on the railway which has a very steep climb after the halt at Kinneil. Also in the picture is a class 27 in green livery and a BR Class 14 diesel hydraulic shunter. This particular one had been in industrial use at the nearby Grangemouth Refinery with BP. The BR blue and TOPS numbering are a livery this loco never carried.

Working hard on the steep climb up to Birkhill on the Bo'ness & Kinneil Railway is Caley tank 419, complete with Caley route indicator (the device in front of the chimney). Birkhill used to be the line's terminus and had a clay mine to investigate. The line now carries on to Manuel adjacent to the Edinburgh to Glasgow line and where the B&KR joins to Network Rail lines.

A view from the currently out of use footbridge at the Boness & Kinneil Railway which shows the site as it then was in 2004 to good effect with signal box, station buildings and engine shed. When the SRPS moved to this site none of these buildings were there. There are other sheds on the site, one incorporating a museum and development continues with new workshop facilities being created. Whilst the main attraction might be 80105, the standard 4MT tank we can also see class 08, 20 and 47 diesels and a "Blue Train" Glasgow area electric unit. I know from working on 80135 and 80136 at North Yorkshire what fine engines the Standard tanks are. On one trip with the full diner set, we were stopped at the signal on the bank just outside Goathland but without a slip 80135 restarted the train, equivalent weight of 9 Mk1s, to proceed into Goathland – I think my driver left the footplate to 'have a word' with the signaller! 80105 is currently undergoing an overhaul.

The SRPS are custodians of *Morayshire*, currently it is undergoing a ten-year overhaul. Prior to preservation, this loco was stored at Edinburgh Dalry Road shed (64C). It has made infrequent visits to other railways during periods in traffic. It has also been turned out in LNER apple green livery but when this photograph was taken BR lined black had been applied. The engine is sitting outside the east end of the engine shed and behind can be seen another of the sheds that have grown up around the site over the years.

The railway's 'Caley tank' number 419 has been a feature of the SRPS fleet along with J36 *Maude*. It has been out shopped in BR black and Caledonian liveries. In 2005 when this picture was taken, 419 was in Caley blue and happily was coupled to the two Caledonian liveried coaches thus making a very pleasing picture.

The connection to the Edinburgh to Glasgow main line at Manuel, but called Bo'ness Junction, allows main line visitors and of course the SRPS rail tour stock access to Network Rail metals. This picture shows two visitors. No 6, an Andrew Barclay 0-4-0, is on a long term loan from East Lothian Council's Prestongrange site. It had worked at several collieries with the NCB including Kinneil and had arrived from Prestongrange by road. The other visitor, West Coast Railway's 46115 *Scots Guardsman* had arrived via Bo'ness Junction and was at the railway for servicing between charters. Having worked on both engines it was fortuitous to be able to picture them together.

Just outside the engine shed at Bo'ness the day before a very well attended gala weekend are the two remaining working Caledonian railway engines both in Caley livery. One is 419 seen earlier but in a rather different shade of blue, the other is 828 which we have also seen before but in BR black at Aviemore as 57566. It is a visitor from the Strathspey Railway to allow the two Caledonian liveried engines to work trains including the Caley liveried coaches. Having the two engines together proved a very compelling lure for enthusiasts.

There is a strong diesel group at Bo'ness and the fleet reflects well the sort of traction that could have been seen in Central Scotland. One of those classes was of course the BRCW 26. The year is 2006 and 26 024 looks almost ex works standing outside the shed on the run round line in the station. The loco had spent spells at Haymarket, Inverness and Eastfield depots before withdrawal in 1992. It was bought for preservation and, after asbestos removal at MC Metals, arrived at Bo'ness. Since this photograph was taken, the loco underwent a further refurbishment, as I recall in Cardiff. I have driven the loco at NYMR.

No 29, an ex NCB 0-4-0 Andrew Barclay tank engine is seen in a play area at Danderhall in 1983. It was not uncommon to find steam engines in similar locations. This particular one suffered from graffiti and vandalism, so a new home had to be found. The loco was first moved to Prestongrange where we began to strip it down and assess what work may be required to bring it back to steam. The overhaul was found to be beyond our resources; however, all was not lost as the loco has since moved to Lathalmond in Fife and progress there has been good. This engine is now very close to returning to steam.

CHAPTER 12
STEAM ON BR

I think my first experience of steam on the National Network was visiting a rail show at Stirling. The SRPS J36 *Maude* was in one of the bay platforms and Sir John Cameron's A4 *Union of South Africa* was supposed to be there but was running late. We did see it fleetingly on the way home.

I suppose that would have been in the early '70s so steam had not been gone for all that long from BR. Perhaps the Scottish Region were more open to steam haulage as there did seem to be quite a few excursions usually using the two engines mentioned above. *Maude* made several circuits of the Edinburgh South suburban line one December Sunday doing 'Santa' trains. I have also seen the same loco in Fife and Central Scotland but being a relatively small engine the length of the trains were limited. The A4 carried out some driver training trips to Perth so that there were steam trained drivers and firemen available for excursions.

Of course, the West Highland line from Fort William was also an early return for steam haulage and what is now 'The Jacobite' is an established tourist attraction. I recall seeing *Flying Scotsman* come into Waverley one Saturday morning, but I confess that we were more interested in a rather rare named Western Region 47 appearing that same day. Happily, the variety of locomotives and routes has expanded over the years and the recent rejuvenation of the Ferryhill turntable has made Aberdeen a viable day trip destination from central Scotland. The Borders line also attracts steam charters and circular tours via the Forth Bridge remain popular. Various 'Great Britain' tours have visited all points of the country using a variety of engines. I was on the support crew for *Galatea* visiting Inverness. The Edinburgh Sub sees a fair amount of steam, although it is a taxing route for the crews, especially coming from Gorgie or Slateford up to the summit at Morningside Road. With the Ryder Cup charter, I think we woke some of the residents of Morningside Cemetery as *Scots Guardsman* tackled the climb up through the cutting at Myreside Road!.

Mainline connections at Aviemore and Bo'ness are very useful for visiting trains and engines, where the latter can be serviced on a depot with its facilities. As a fan of Stanier engines I have been very pleased to see Duchesses on their home turf of the WCML and Black 5s on the Highland Main Line. Perhaps the highlight so far was being on the footplate of *Scots Guardsman* attacking Beattock under the control of Driver Gordon Hodgson, an ex Carlisle Canal and Kingmoor driver, with Fireman Chris Holmes providing the steam and shovelling all but continuously.

There is little doubt that the sight and sound of a steam engine remains a lure for enthusiasts and the general public alike.

As Sir John Cameron's A4 has had to retire prematurely, it is appropriate to look at a selection of views of *Union of South Africa* in happier times. The first of these is taken on the Edinburgh Sub looking up to the railway at the Cameron Toll roundabout. There are two bridges over either side of the roundabout, and they have been refurbished over the years. Behind the photographer is the Cameron Toll shopping centre. Since the time this was taken, trees have grown so it isn't possible to recreate this view today. I noticed the whistle is being blown, so perhaps Sir John is on the footplate.

Still on the Sub, the A4 is climbing from Blackford Hill to Morningside Road and is doing well. At this point, the bottom of Cluny Avenue, the railway is almost at road level and now is a Network Rail access point. This piece of railway is a tricky one for crews given the incline and there is a signal a few hundred yards ahead. This is the same stretch of line that we saw the Western negotiating. When I first moved to Edinburgh there was still an LNER trespass notice attached to a rail as a post on the embankment just a wee bit back up the road from where this picture was taken.

This time we are at Craiglockhart Junction. The A4 has just passed under a road and the Union Canal, the wooden structure above the tunnel portal being the boat house of local school George Watson's College. The A4 heads straight on for Gorgie Junction which would allow the train to head east to Haymarket and Waverley or west onto the lines for Fife or Glasgow. The lines that diverge take you to Slateford and lines west, including those to Cobbinshaw and Carstairs.

This time the A4 and support coach is at rest in Waverley Station and sporting a different nameplate. It is 1990 and *Osprey*, the name originally intended for the engine, is in use due to political circumstances in South Africa. Note the vehicle in the background as these were the motorail platforms. Sadly 'Number 9' is unlikely to visit Waverley again in steam or otherwise. The station roof has been completed re-glazed since and of course the track plan has altered dramatically too.

This is the picture that I struggled to work out from where I had taken it. The backdrop is Haymarket shed and the K1 has come from Haymarket Central Junction thus heading for Gorgie and the Sub. What the tour was eludes me and I must have been standing on part of the Western Approach Road heading from Dalry to Murrayfield, which follows the route of the Caley line from Princes Street. Indeed, the Western Approach Road follows the route from Lothian Road and as you fork right to take the road over Dalry Road and down to Murrayfield stadium you drive over the site of 64C Dalry Road shed.

The same locomotive in immaculate condition, note the squared off buffers, but this time on the West Highland Line heading south from Fort William and Mallaig. The train was along the lines of the *Royal Scotsman* and also had an observation car. As can be seen, there is still a fair amount of snow on the mountains and this was a crisp and rather cold day. I had watched the train approach Rannoch, over the viaduct and through the stunning landscape. Rannoch is a passing point as can be seen from the carriage on the other side of the platform. All seems to be well, the steam heat is working, the safety valves are lifting, plenty of steam but, oh, dear, that chimney will not do. Were I to produce such an effect at the Moors I would be in serious bother. I have fired this loco at Grosmont but it is currently in BR black livery. The loco remains active in the West Highlands as a regular on 'The Jacobite'.

The SRPS's J36 *Maude* in NB livery takes water at Stirling; mind you, the engine is doing its best to use the water as quickly as it goes into the tender. As I recall this spectacular blowing off at the safety valves went on for some time. Somewhere along the line the fireman had been over enthusiastic with the shovel. Whilst the engine is gloriously sunlit, the clouds suggest that rain is not far away and it wasn't! *Maude* was a very busy engine out and about on the main line in those days but given its size and power output I wonder if Network Rail would be able to allow it out and about again.

Maude again. Also in sunshine which this time lasted most of the day. The location is Cameron Toll, we saw the A4 on the first of the overbridges and this is the second, which have seen bridge strikes from buses and lorries. There used to be an over-height warning system at this location. Given the clear sky and visible exhaust I think this may have been one of the Santa Specials that were run as a circular trip from Waverley round the Sub. These were run from the Sub platforms and there were several each day. A fine idea but I suspect that Waverley would no longer have the capacity to allow this to run today.

Another loco that I have fired is *Blue Peter*. It has been out of traffic for some years but is on the way back now. Here the engine is very much on its old stomping ground as a Dundee Tay Bridge loco. This is North Queensferry and the train has just crossed the Forth Bridge and is about to descend to Inverkeithing. From my experience this is a very strong engine and made short work of the climb out of Grosmont, if of course you had properly prepared your fire and with a wide fire box that is quite a lot of coal. I wonder what was going through the mind of the gent sitting astride the footbridge.

This is a 1985 picture and I think the loco is using the triangle at Inverkeithing to turn. The Black 5, 44767 was fitted with Stephenson Link motion instead of the usual Walschaerts valve gear. Once again, I have worked with this loco at NYMR. The engine has changed hands since and has been out of action for some years; however, it is now at Carnforth and a return to main line work is on the cards.

The same engine, this time on West Highland duties heading for Mallaig. Compare the almost invisible haze at the chimney with the rather more obvious output from the K1. For a while, the West Highland line coaches were painted green and white rather than blue and white and that colour scheme also found its way to the Kyle line. The zoom lens has been put to work here and, to my mind anyway, shows the very fine lines of a Black 5. But then perhaps my view is biased as I am a fan of these locos.

Back at Edinburgh Waverley on the Sub platforms in April of 1985 and we find another of Stanier's designs this time Jubilee 5690 *Leander* in LMS crimson lake livery. This was a bitterly cold day and the engine was hauling a charter to Fife, indeed I think that 44767 was involved in hauling the same trip. Happily, *Leander* is still very much on the go on the main line and I have been on the footplate between Carlisle and Appleby.

Keeping up the Stanier theme we see what has been described as his 'masterpiece' a Duchess. This is *Duchess of Sutherland* in BR green and has come from Winchburgh to Dalmeny Junction. Once under the bridge I have taken the photograph from the train will go through Dalmeny Station and then across the Forth Bridge. The cab layout of these machines is very similar to that on a 5, a jubilee or an 8F, just much bigger! So much vegetation has grown up that you would need to spend some time with a pair of shears to obtain this particular viewpoint today.

The other preserved Duchess that used to be on the main line was 46229 *Duchess of Hamilton.* It is of course now streamlined and on display at York. The engine is on familiar territory here as it takes water at Abington loop on the West Coast Main Line. The coal pusher is in use, evidenced by the plume of steam at the back of the tender. This device must have been very much welcomed by the crews working these fine, but hungry, engines. I have fired and driven this engine at the Mid Hants Railway on a driver experience course. I am very glad I decided to do that as that is the only time I have been able to work one of these excellent engines. The hydrant the support crew were using must have been some distance off as several lines of hose were used. Rolling them out isn't too hard but rolling them up is a different story!

Despite the 'Royal Scot' headboard *Duchess of Hamilton* is on the East Coast main Line in 1997. The third Duchess that remains is *City of Birmingham*, in original BR paintwork but it is a museum piece only. Thus *Duchess of Sutherland* is the sole representative of the class that is still active. The firebox on these engines is massive and to get a good back end in, absolutely essential if you want to get anywhere, takes a lot of coal and effort, well over 100 shovelfuls and then to keep that topped up on the road is no mean feat. Seeing the size of the task and having a go at it puts into perspective the efforts of Duchess firemen and how arduous the Crewe to Perth workings must have been and what a blessing the steam coal pusher was.

The J36 *Maude* was a much used engine out and about on BR, as it then was, however as a small engine it sometimes needed a little help to keep time and climb gradients. This was one such occasion and a class 26 (if the stag transfer is correct an Inverness engine) is piloting. I am fairly sure this was in Fife and the 26 came off to allow *Maude* to proceed solo. All that said, *Maude* was used for Santa trains round the Edinburgh Sub without assistance, not the easiest of roads for engine or crew.

Some all too typical West Highland weather at, I think, Arisaig where I found B1 61264 returning to Fort William from Mallaig. This is a 2005 image and shows the variety of engines that have, over the years, worked 'The Jacobite'. This is another engine that I have fired at NYMR. Being an LNER engine it has a letter box flap fire-hole door and with the shape of the fire grate, which is level from the door but then slopes down to the front of the firebox, you have to put a lot more down the front than on say a BR Standard. A proper Lucas shovel, half shovelfuls and accuracy should enable the fireman to maintain boiler pressure and water levels. If you don't get it right, the needle will drop as will the water level. Personally, I am not a great fan of the letterbox fire-hole door.

The Great Britain rail-tours take steam to all points of the country. The date of this picture eludes me, but it was taken at 15:08 and 14 seconds according to the station clock. This is Dunkeld and a few photographers have turned out to see leading a Black 5 piloting an LNE loco, and I fear I cannot recall of which class. Text book 'chimneys' on both locos, just a haze of light smoke but as there is quite a stiff climb out of Dunkeld heading south both locos would soon be opened up. I have fired this section of line on Jubilee *Galatea* and I didn't look out to see if there were photographers on the station as I was busy with the shovel!

An old friend, 60007 *Sir Nigel Gresley*. I have fired and driven this loco many times at North Yorkshire and knew the late Roger Barker, the loco's 'minder' very well. This photograph shows off the A4's elegant lines and the roof of the corridor in the tender on the right hand side. The engine is taking water between Dalmeny and Winchburgh, the support crew will have rolled out four lines of hose to reach the hydrant. I know that because we took water here with *Scots Guardsman* returning from Thornton after working the Ryder Cup charter. As there are no wires to be seen we also took the opportunity to get a good supply of coal raked down for the fireman.

A Scot on Beattock! Nothing unusual with that in the 1960s however this is many years later and 46115 *Scots Guardsman* is on 'Great Britain' duties; all must be going well on the footplate, feathering at the safety valve and the smoke shows that a round has just been put on or perhaps the firing is almost continuous. I had managed to get a day off work to go and see the GB and I am perched up a hillside beside the old main road, little used since the A74M was built. We were treated to two steam workings that afternoon as two of Ian Riley's Black 5s had headed north engines and support coach before the GB arrived. The Scot was certainly working hard, its beat echoing off the surrounding hills.

We are back at Gleneagles to see another 'Great Britain' tour, this time with double headed Black 5s 45231 and 45407 heading for Perth and then, I think, Inverness. Now some will say that I should have let the train come further before releasing the shutter and I take the point. However, not only did I want to get a photograph of the Black 5s, I also wanted to wave to the fireman on the leading engine, my good friend, emporium owner and raconteur the late John Fletcher. Happily, I managed both!

It is the end of the line for K1, 2005 as it has reached the buffer stops at Mallaig, just as we have reached the end of our journey round Scotland. As we can see the K1 is in its LNER apple green livery and the crew are having a chat with some of the train staff. Also in the picture, but only just is the observation car which formed part of this charter. The views from the observation car must have been quite spectacular as this was a very fine day. With the charter train market expanding, I do wonder if we will see observation cars again. The GW saloon at the Moors certainly sees plenty of use. As there is no longer a turntable at Mallaig, the K1 will return to Fort William tender first. Of course, the turntable used to be used to turn the observation car too. I hope you have enjoyed your trip with me.